D0615395

THE HUMAN BODY
How It Works

Cells, Tissues, and Skin

THE HUMAN BODY
How It Works

THE HUMAN BODY
How It Works

Cells, Tissues, and Skin

Douglas B. Light

INTRODUCTION BY
Denton A. Cooley, M.D.
President and Surgeon-in-Chief
of the Texas Heart Institute
Clinical Professor of Surgery at the
University of Texas Medical School, Houston, Texas

CHELSEA HOUSE
PUBLISHERS
An imprint of Infobase Publishing

Chelsea House
An imprint of Infobase Publishing
132 West 31st Street
New York NY 10001

Library of Congress Cataloging-in-Publication Data

Light, Douglas B., 1956-
  Cells, tissues, and skin / Douglas Light.
    p. cm. -- (The human body: how it works)
  Includes bibliographical references and index.
  ISBN 978-1-60413-370-7 (hardcover)
  1. Cells--Juvenile literature. 2. Tissues--Juvenile literature. 3. Skin--Juvenile literature. I. Title. II. Series.
  QH582.5.L522 2009
  611'.018--dc22
                                2008052559

Chelsea House books are available at special discounts when purchased in bulk quantities for businesses, associations, institutions, or sales promotions. Please call our Special Sales Department in New York at (212) 967-8800 or (800) 322-8755.

You can find Chelsea House on the World Wide Web at
http://www.chelseahouse.com

Series design by Erika Arroyo, Erik Lindstrom
Cover design by Takeshi Takahashi

Printed in the United States of America

Bang EJB 10 9 8 7 6 5 4 3 2

This book is printed on acid-free paper.

All links and Web addresses were checked and verified to be correct at the time of publication. Because of the dynamic nature of the Web, some addresses and links may have changed since publication and may no longer be valid.

Contents

Introduction

THE HUMAN BODY IS AN INCREDIBLY COMPLEX AND amazing structure. At best, it is a source of strength, beauty, and wonder. We can compare the healthy body to a well-designed machine whose parts work smoothly together. We can also compare it to a symphony orchestra in which each instrument has a different part to play. When all of the musicians play together, they produce beautiful music.

From a purely physical standpoint, our bodies are made mainly of water. We are also made of many minerals, including calcium, phosphorous, potassium, sulfur, sodium, chlorine, magnesium, and iron. In order of size, the elements of the body are organized into cells, tissues, and organs. Related organs are combined into systems, including the musculo-skeletal, cardiovascular, nervous, respiratory, gastrointestinal, endocrine, and reproductive systems.

Our cells and tissues are constantly wearing out and being replaced without our even knowing it. In fact, much of the time, we take the body for granted. When it is working properly, we tend to ignore it. Although the heart beats about 100,000 times per day and we breathe more than 10 million times per year, we do not normally think about these things. When something goes wrong, however, our bodies tell us through pain and other symptoms. In fact, pain is a very effective alarm system that lets us know the body needs attention. If the pain does not go away, we may need to see a doctor. Even without medical help, the body has an amazing ability to heal itself. If we cut ourselves, the blood-clotting system works to seal the cut right away, and the immune defense system sends out special blood cells that are pro-grammed to heal the area.

During the past 50 years, doctors have gained the ability to repair or replace almost every part of the body. In my own field of cardiovascular surgery, we are able to open the heart and repair its valves, arteries, chambers, and connections. In many cases, these repairs can be done through a tiny "keyhole" incision that speeds up patient recovery and leaves hardly any scar. If the entire heart is diseased, we can replace it altogether, either with a donor heart or with a mechanical device. In the future, the use of mechanical hearts will probably be common in patients who would otherwise die of heart disease.

Until the mid-twentieth century, infections and contagious diseases related to viruses and bacteria were the most common causes of death. Even a simple scratch could become infected and lead to death from "blood poisoning." After penicillin and other antibiotics became available in the 1930s and 1940s, doc-tors were able to treat blood poisoning, tuberculosis, pneumo-nia, and many other bacterial diseases. Also, the introduction of modern vaccines allowed us to prevent childhood illnesses, smallpox, polio, flu, and other contagions that used to kill or cripple thousands.

Today, plagues such as the "Spanish flu" epidemic of 1918–19, which killed 20 to 40 million people worldwide, are unknown except in history books. Now that these diseases can be avoided, people are living long enough to have long-term (chronic) conditions such as cancer, heart failure, diabetes, and arthritis. Because chronic diseases tend to involve many organ systems or even the whole body, they cannot always be cured with surgery. These days, researchers are doing a lot of work at the cellular level, trying to find the underlying causes of chronic illnesses. Scientists recently finished mapping the human genome, which is a set of coded "instructions" programmed into our cells. Each cell contains 3 billion "letters" of this code. By showing how the body is made, the human genome will help researchers prevent and treat disease at its source, within the cells themselves.

The body's long-term health depends on many factors, called risk factors. Some risk factors, including our age, sex, and family history of certain diseases, are beyond our control. Other important risk factors include our lifestyle, behavior, and environment. Our modern lifestyle offers many advantages but is not always good for our bodies. In western Europe and the United States, we tend to be stressed, overweight, and out of shape. Many of us have unhealthy habits such as smoking cigarettes, abusing alcohol, or using drugs. Our air, water, and food often contain hazardous chemicals and industrial waste products. Fortunately, we can do something about most of these risk factors. At any age, the most important things we can do for our bodies are to eat right, exercise regularly, get enough sleep, and refuse to smoke, overuse alcohol, or use addictive drugs. We can also help clean up our environment. These simple steps will lower our chances of getting cancer, heart disease, or other serious disorders.

These days, thanks to the Internet and other forms of media coverage, people are more aware of health-related matters. The average person knows more about the human body than ever before. Patients want to understand their medical conditions and treatment options. They want to play a more active role, along with their doctors, in making medical decisions and in taking care of their own health.

I encourage you to learn as much as you can about your body and to treat your body well. These things may not seem too important to you now, while you are young, but the habits and behaviors that you practice today will affect your physical well-being for the rest of your life. The present book series, YOUR BODY: HOW IT WORKS, is an excellent introduction to human biology and anatomy. I hope that it will awaken within you a lifelong interest in these subjects.

Denton A. Cooley, M.D.
President and Surgeon-in-Chief
of the Texas Heart Institute
Clinical Professor of Surgery at the
University of Texas Medical School, Houston, Texas

1

Cells: The Basis of Life

Cells ARE THE BASIC UNITS OF STRUCTURE AND FUNCTION IN ALL living organisms. Some organisms, such as bacteria and protozoa, consist of only a single cell. In contrast, complex organisms like human beings are composed of over 75 trillion cells. Just one drop of human blood contains about 5 million red blood cells.

CELLS VARY WIDELY IN SIZE AND SHAPE

Although most cells are microscopic, they do vary in size. For instance, sperm cells are only about 1/12,000th of an inch (about 2 **micrometers**, or μm) long, whereas some nerve cells are over 3 feet (1 meter, or m) in length (for example, a single nerve cell connects the spinal cord in your lower back to the little toe).

Cells also vary in shape, which reflects their particular function. *Nerve cells*, for example, typically have long, threadlike extensions that transmit impulses from one part of the body to another. *Epithelial cells*, which compose the outer layers of the skin, can be flattened and tightly packed like floor tiles, forming a protective layer for underlying cells. *Muscle cells* are designed to generate force by contracting, or shortening. The shape of the cells depends on the particular kind of muscle. *Red blood cells*, which carry oxygen from the lungs to virtually every cell in the body, are **biconcave** and disk-shaped (Figure 1.1), whereas some kidney cells resemble a cube. All in all, the human body has over 200 different types of cells.

THE DISCOVERY OF CELLS

Because of their small size, the discovery of cells and their structure had to wait for the invention of the compound microscope, which occurred in the late sixteenth century (Zacharias Jansen, a Dutch optician, is usually given credit for the first compound microscope). During the mid-seventeenth century, the English scientist Robert Hooke looked at thinly sliced cork with a simple microscope. He observed tiny compartments, which he termed *cellulae*, the Latin word for small rooms; hence the origin of the biological term *cell* (technically speaking, he actually observed the walls of dead plant cells, but no one at that time thought of cells as being dead or alive). In the late seventeenth century, the Dutch shopkeeper Anton van Leeuwenhoek constructed lenses that provided clarity and magnification that was not previously possible. With these new lenses, he observed very small "animalcules" in scrapings of tartar from his own teeth, as well as protozoa from a variety of water samples.

In the early nineteenth century, the German botanist Matthias Schleiden, who also studied cells with a microscope, proposed that the **nucleus** might have something to do with cell development. During the same time period, the German zoologist Theodor Schwann theorized that animals and plants consist of cells and that cells have an individual life of their own. Rudolf Virchow, a German physiologist who studied cell growth and reproduction, suggested all cells come from preexisting cells. His proposal was actually revolutionary for the time because it challenged the widely accepted theory of **spontaneous generation**, which held that living organisms arise spontaneously from nonliving material such as garbage.

By the middle of the nineteenth century, the scientific community developed several important principles that today

Figure 1.1   Red blood cells are only one of more than 200 different types of cells in the body. The biconcave disk form of red blood cells allows them to carry oxygen efficiently and their flexibility allows them to squeeze through narrow blood vessels.

make up the **cell theory**. The first of these principles is that every living organism is composed of one or more cells. The second is that cells are the smallest units that have all the properties of life. The third is that all cells come from preexisting cells.

Microscopes

Modern microscopes have dramatically increased our ability to observe cell structure. **Light microscopes** use two or more

CELL THEORY

Until the nineteenth century, it was generally accepted that a number of living organisms arose spontaneously from nonliving matter by a process termed spontaneous generation. For instance, it was assumed that maggots arose from rotting meat and mice from rotting grain. Through a series of controlled experiments by a number of scientists, including Francesco Redi, John Needham, Lazzaro Spallanzani, and Louis Pasteur, the theory of spontaneous generation was finally refuted in 1859. The cell theory, developed in the mid-nineteenth century, provided scientists with a clearer insight of the study of life. It was formally articulated in 1839 by Matthias Schleiden and Theodor Schwann and has remained a paradigm of modern biology. The cell theory involves the following aspects:

- Every known living organism is composed of one or more cells, the structural and functional units of all living things.
- Cells are the smallest units that have the characteristics of life (e.g., they exhibit a complex and highly ordered organization, use and transform energy, reproduce, grow and develop, and regulate their internal environment).
- All cells come from preexisting cells. That is, the continuity of life has a cellular basis, and spontaneous generation does not occur.
- Cells contain hereditary information (DNA) that is passed along during cell division.
- The chemical composition of all cells is essentially the same.
- All metabolism in living organisms occurs within cells.

sets of highly polished glass lenses to bend light rays to illuminate a specimen, thereby enlarging its image. Consequently, in
order to be seen, a specimen must be thin enough for light to
pass through it. Also, cells are 60% to 80% water, which is colorless and clear. This, in turn, makes it difficult to observe the
various unpigmented structures of cells. This problem can be
overcome by exposing cells to **stains** (dyes), which color some
cell parts but not others.

Unfortunately, staining usually kills cells. However, there
are different types of microscopes that refract light to create
contrast without staining. These microscopes use *phase-con-
trast* or *Nomarksi optics*. With Nomarski optics, for example, a
beam of polarized light is split in two by a prism, and then both
beams are projected through a specimen at slightly different
angles. When the beams are later combined, they exhibit bright
and dark interference patterns that highlight areas in cells having differing thicknesses. Such specialized optics obviously
enhance the usefulness of light microscopes.

Two factors need to be considered when discussing
microscopy: first, a microscope's ability to *magnify* images and,
second, its ability to *resolve* them. Magnification simply means
making an image appear larger in size. **Resolution**, a measure of
clarity, refers to the ability of a microscope to show as separate
two points that are close together. If a microscope magnified an
image without providing sufficient resolution, the image would
be large but not sharp.

The human eye cannot resolve details smaller than about
0.0039 inches (0.1 millimeter, or mm), whereas the resolution
of a light microscope is about 500 times greater, making it
possible to observe objects the size of small bacteria. Nonetheless, light microscopes have an inherent limitation regarding
resolution because of the physical nature of light. Light, a
form of **electromagnetic radiation**, has wavelike properties. The
wavelength refers to the distance between two wave crests (red
light, for example, has a longer wavelength than violet light;
750 **nanometers** versus 400 nanometers, respectively). If a cell

structure is less than one-half the wavelength of the illuminating light, it will not affect the light rays streaming through it. In other words, it will be invisible. As a result, light microscopes are not useful for observing objects smaller than several hundred nanometers.

Electron microscopes have much greater magnifying and resolving powers because they use a beam of electrons to "illuminate" a specimen instead of light. Although electrons are particles, they also have wavelike properties, and a stream of electrons has a wavelength about 100,000 times shorter than that of visible light. This allows an electron microscope to resolve images down to about 0.5 nanometers in size. However, because a beam of electrons cannot pass through glass, its path is focused by a magnetic field. In addition, specimens must be placed in a vacuum; otherwise molecules of air would deflect the electron beam.

There are two main kinds of electron microscopes. A **transmission electron microscope**, or TEM, accelerates a beam of electrons through a specimen, which allows structures within a cell to be imaged (Figure 1.2a). In contrast, a **scanning electron microscope**, or SEM, moves a narrow beam of electrons across a specimen that has been coated with a thin layer of metal. This method is ideally suited for imaging the surface of a specimen (Figure 1.2b).

CHEMICAL CONSTITUENTS OF CELLS

Chemically, cells are mainly composed of four **elements**: carbon, hydrogen, oxygen, and nitrogen. Although these four **major elements** make up over 95% of a cell's structure, the **trace elements**, which are present in much smaller amounts, also are important for certain cell functions (Figure 1.3). Iron, for instance, is needed to make **hemoglobin**, the red pigment that carries oxygen in the blood. Blood clotting, muscle function, and the proper formation of bones and teeth all require calcium. Iodine is necessary to make thyroid hormone, which controls the body's metabolic rate. A lack of iodine in the

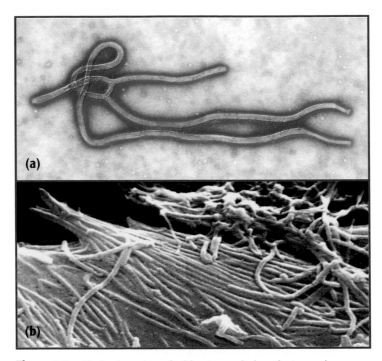

Figure 1.2   Ebola virus viewed with a transmission electron microscope (TEM) (a) and with a scanning electron microscope (SEM) (b).

diet can lead to the formation of a *goiter* (an enlarged thyroid gland). Although goiters were relatively common in the past, they are less common today because dietary iodine can be obtained through the consumption of iodized salt. Sodium and potassium are also necessary elements, especially for the transmission of nerve impulses and for muscle contraction.

Chemical compounds are classified as organic or inorganic. **Organic compounds** are those that contain carbon and hydrogen atoms. All other are classified as **inorganic**. The most abundant inorganic compound in cells, and in the body as a whole, is water. In fact, water accounts for about two-thirds of an adult human's weight. This helps explain why water is essential for life. Water is important as a **solvent** because many substances, called **solutes**, dissolve in it. Also, water helps stabilize body

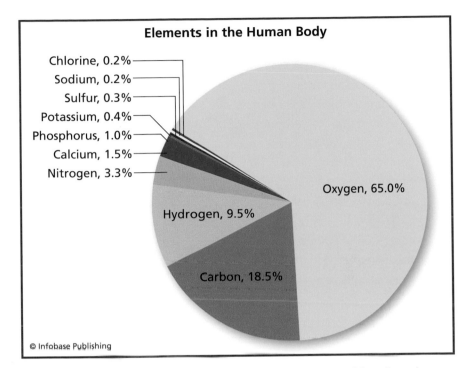

Elements in the Human Body

Chlorine, 0.2%
Sodium, 0.2%
Sulfur, 0.3%
Potassium, 0.4%
Phosphorus, 1.0%
Calcium, 1.5%
Nitrogen, 3.3%

Oxygen, 65.0%

Hydrogen, 9.5%

Carbon, 18.5%

© Infobase Publishing

Figure 1.3 Some of the more common elements found in cells and their approximate amounts. Oxygen, carbon, hydrogen, and nitrogen are all important components of cells and make up over 90% of a cell's structure. Calcium, phosphorus, and potassium are also found in cells, but in much smaller amounts and are known as trace elements.

temperature because, compared to many fluids, it can absorb a lot of heat before its temperature rises, and cells release a great amount of heat during normal **metabolism**. In addition to water, other inorganic substances found in cells include oxygen, carbon dioxide, and numerous inorganic salts such as sodium chloride (ordinary table salt).

Organic substances in cells include **carbohydrates**, **lipids**, **proteins**, and **nucleic acids**. Carbohydrates in the form of sugars, such as glucose, sucrose, glycogen, and starch, provide much of the energy that cells require. The chemical reactions these compounds release break down and their energy is part of metabolism, the sum total of all the chemical reactions in the body. Carbohydrates also provide materials to build certain cell structures. Lipids are insoluble in water and include compounds such as fats (triglycerides), **phospholipids**, and **cholesterol**. Fats serve primarily as energy storage compounds; phospholipids are an important constituent of cell membranes; and cholesterol is an important component of steroid hormones, such as testosterone and estrogen, and is also a structural part of cell membranes. Proteins are composed of amino acids and function as structural materials, **enzymes**, and hormones. Enzymes act as catalysts that increase the rate of chemical reactions. Other proteins are found in antibodies, hemoglobin, and the contractile compounds of muscle. Nucleic acids, known as **RNA (ribonucleic acid)** and **DNA (deoxyribonucleic acid)**, make up the genetic material in all living organisms.

STRUCTURE OF A GENERALIZED CELL

There are two major types of cells distinguished on the basis of structure. Bacteria are prokaryotic cells, whereas all other life forms (protists, fungi, plants, and animals) are made of eukaryotic cells. All cells, prokaryotic and eukaryotic, are surrounded by a **plasma membrane**, which is a thin outer boundary that separates the intracellular environment from the extracellular one. The plasma membrane maintains cells as entities that are physically distinct from their environment. To do this, they must control which substances enter and leave the cell.

All cells also have **genes** made of DNA, which is hereditary material, and **ribosomes**, tiny structures that help make proteins (a further description of ribosomes is given in Chapter 4). However, only eukaryotic cells have a membrane-enclosed nucleus.

Although eukaryotic cells differ from one another in many respects, they all have certain characteristics and structures in common. Consequently, it is possible to construct a generalized, or composite, cell (Figure 1.4). It is noteworthy to consider the complex organization of a eukaryotic cell. The

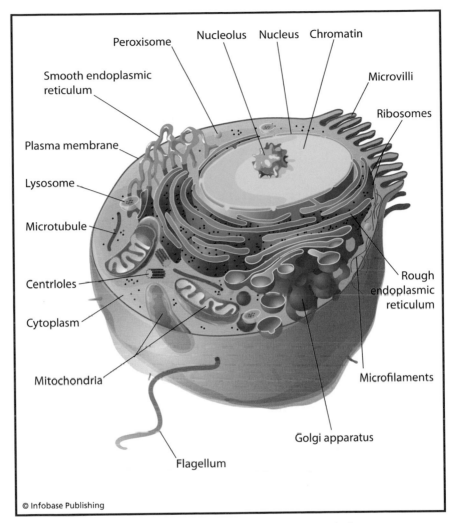

Figure 1.4 This composite cell illustrates some of the common features and organization of many cell types. However, it does not give an idea of the great diversity in size, shape, and structure among cells, which reflects their different functions. Note the many organelles, which perform specific functions, thereby allowing the cell to survive and perform particular tasks.

most obvious **organelle** seen with a microscope is the nucleus. There is one notable exception, however. Mature mammalian red blood cells do not possess a nucleus. The nucleus contains the heritable genetic material called deoxyribonucleic acid (DNA) and molecules of ribonucleic acid (RNA) that are able to copy instructions from DNA in order for a cell to synthesize proteins.

In addition, cells contain a semifluid **cytoplasm** (this term is used for the interior of both prokaryotic and eukaryotic cells). The cytoplasm fills the cell between the nucleus and the plasma membrane. Cytoplasm contains specialized structures called organelles, which are suspended in a liquid **cytosol**. The various types of organelles perform specific cell functions. Whereas organelles divide the labor of a cell, the nucleus directs overall cell activities.

Levels of Structural Organization

Single-celled organisms (prokaryotes, protists, and some fungi, such as yeast) have the ability to carry out all necessary life functions as individual cells. For example, they can obtain and digest food, eliminate waste products, and respond to a number of different stimuli. However, in multicellular organisms such as human beings, cells do not generally operate independently. Instead, they display highly specialized functions, and only by living and communicating with other cells do they allow the entire organism to survive.

Groups of cells that are similar in structure and perform a common function are called **tissues**. There are four main tissue types in the human body: *epithelial, connective, muscle,* and *nervous*. Each performs a different role (a further discussion of tissues is presented in Chapter 6). The study of tissues is called **histology**, and scientists who specialize in this field are called histologists. Physicians who study tissues removed from a patient during an operation or from a person during a postmortem examination are called *pathologists*, and they look at the cells with a microscope to help diagnose the presence of specific diseases. **Cancer**, for instance, is detected in this manner.

Tissues can be organized into more complex structures called **organs**, which perform specific functions for the body. Some examples of organs include the kidneys, lungs, stomach, liver, and skin. Many organs, such as the small intestine and skin, are composed of all four tissue types. The small intestine, for instance, is capable of digesting and absorbing food, which requires the cooperation of a number of different kinds of cells and tissue types.

An **organ** system is a group of organs that cooperate to accomplish a common purpose. An example is the digestive system, which contains a number of organs, including the

WHY ARE CELLS SMALL?

Why are most cells microscopic in size? It turns out that there are physical constraints on cell size that are determined by their *surface area to volume ratio*. This is because an object's volume increases with the cube of its radius, while its surface area increases only with the square of the radius. In other words, as a cell grows in size, the volume increases much faster than the surface area. For example, if a cell increases by four times in diameter, its volume increases by 64 times (4^3), but its surface area increases only by 16 times (4^2). In this example, the plasma membrane would therefore have to serve four times as much cytoplasm as it had previously. Thus, if a cell were to grow unchecked, it would soon reach a point where the inward flow of nutrients and outward flow of waste products across the plasma membrane could not occur at a sufficient rate to keep the cell alive.

The importance of a large surface area is also seen in the numerous infoldings and outfoldings of the plasma membrane in many cell types (e.g., **microvilli**). These folds dramatically increase the surface area of the plasma membrane relative to cell volume. This is especially important for cells that absorb large quantities of substances, such as those that line the small intestine and many cells in the kidneys.

esophagus, stomach, and small intestine. The **integumentary system** (skin and its accessory structures) is discussed in Chapter 7. All the organ systems of the body make up the complete organism.

CONNECTIONS

Cells are the basic units of structure and function of all living organisms. Although most cells are microscopic, cells do vary widely in size. They also vary in shape, which reflects their particular function. Through investigation of cells, scientists have developed the cell theory, which proposes that (1) all living organisms are composed of one or more cells, (2) cells are the smallest units that have the properties of life, and (3) the continuity of life has a cellular basis (all cells come from preexisting cells).

Chemically, cells are mainly composed of four elements (carbon, hydrogen, oxygen, and nitrogen) and some trace elements (sodium, potassium, calcium, and iron). The most abundant inorganic compound in cells is water. Organic compounds in cells include carbohydrates, lipids, proteins, and nucleic acids. In addition, all human cells start out with three structures in common: a plasma membrane, a nucleus, and cytoplasmic organelles.

Groups of cells that are similar in structure and perform a common or related function are called tissues. Tissues can be organized into more complex structures called organs. An organ system is a group of organs that function together to carry out a specific function, and all the organ systems of the body make up a complete organism.

2

Cell Membranes: Biological Barriers

ALL CELLS ARE SURROUNDED BY A MEMBRANE THAT SERVES as a barrier between the cell's interior contents and the surrounding environment. The membrane that encloses the cell is called the **plasma membrane**, or cell membrane. In addition, most organelles, tiny structures in the cell cytoplasm, are also enclosed by similar membranes. Regardless of location, the membranes are much more than simple boundaries. In fact, they are an actively functioning part of living cells, and many important chemical reactions take place on their inner and outer surfaces.

GENERAL CHARACTERISTICS OF CELL MEMBRANES

In spite of their extreme importance, cell membranes are actually quite fragile and thin. They are typically 7 to 8 nanometers thick (about 10,000 times thinner than a strand of hair), and thus are visible only with the aid of an electron microscope. In addition to maintaining cell integrity, the plasma membrane also controls the movement of many substances into and out of the cell. Because cell membranes have the ability to let some substances through but not others, they are referred to as **selectively permeable**, or **semipermeable**. The permeability properties of the plasma membrane depend on a healthy, intact cell. When cells are damaged, their membranes may become leaky, allowing a number of substances to flow freely across them. For instance, when a person has been severely burned, there can be significant loss of fluids, proteins, and ions from dead and damaged cells in the burned areas.

Membrane Structure

Cell membranes must not only provide a structurally stable boundary, they also need to be flexible, semipermeable, water insoluble, and self-reparable. The basic structural framework of all cell membrane is a double layer, or **bilayer**, of phospholipid molecules (Figure 2.1b). In addition to the phospholipids, protein and cholesterol molecules are dispersed within the membrane layers (Figure 2.1c).

A close inspection of the structural properties of phospholipid molecules is key to understanding how a lipid bilayer forms and how it provides a structurally stable boundary. Each phospholipid molecule has a **phosphate group** and two **fatty acids** chains bound to a three-carbon *glycerol* molecule, making the whole thing look like a lollipop with two sticks (Figure 2.1a).

Phosphate groups are **polar** (meaning charged), making that end of the phospholipid molecule **hydrophilic** (water-soluble). In contrast, the fatty acid regions are **nonpolar** (that is, uncharged), rendering the other portion of the phospholipid **hydrophobic** (water insoluble). The term *amphipathic* is used to describe molecules, such as phospholipids, that have both hydrophilic and hydrophobic regions.

Because water is a major component of both cytoplasm and extracellular fluid, the polar phosphate groups orient themselves so that they lie on both the inner and outer surfaces of a bilayer (Figure 2.1c). In contrast, the nonpolar fatty acid "tails" are lined up in the center of the membrane, sandwiched between the polar "heads." The result is a bilayer composed of two parallel sheets of phospholipid molecules

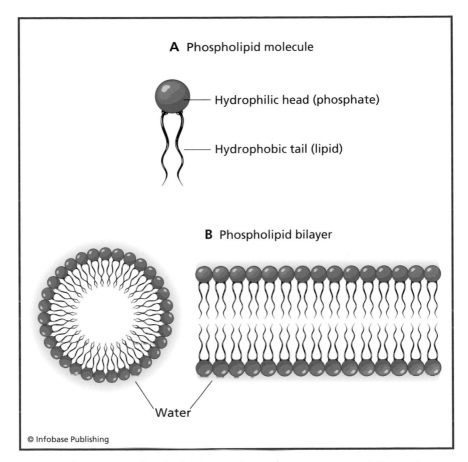

A Phospholipid molecule

Hydrophilic head (phosphate)

Hydrophobic tail (lipid)

B Phospholipid bilayer

Water

© Infobase Publishing

Figure 2.1 Phospholipids are the main components of the cell membrane. (a) A phospholipid is composed of a phosphate group and two fatty acid chains bonded to a glyercol molecule. (b) In a phospholipid bilayer, the polar, hydrophilic heads are arranged toward the inner and outer surfaces of the cell while the fatty acid tails are found on the inside of the membrane. Plasma membranes contain cholesterol, glycolipids, carbohydrates, and protein molecules within the lipid bilayer.

arranged as mirror images. In this way, the two layers lie tail to tail, exposing the polar heads to water. This self-orienting property of phospholipids in an aqueous environment allows cell membranes to self-assemble and also to repair themselves quickly. In fact, the ability of membranes to reseal if torn enables scientists to remove or replace a cell's nucleus during cloning experiments.

About 10% of the outer-facing layer of the membrane is composed of **glycolipids**, lipids with sugar groups attached to them (Figure 2.1c). About 20% of the lipid in membranes is cholesterol. Cholesterol stabilizes the overall structure of a membrane by wedging itself between the phospholipid tails, which also makes membranes less fluid. Interestingly, the amount of cholesterol in membranes can vary depending on the needed level of fluidity (viscosity). Membrane fluidity can also be altered by changes in the relative proportions of saturated and unsaturated fatty acid chains in the phospholipid molecules. Saturated hydrocarbons contain no double bonds. In contrast, unsaturated fatty acids contain one or more double bonds, which puts a kink in the molecule. This in turn prevents tight packing of the fatty acid chains and increases membrane fluidity.

As described above, a lipid bilayer is well suited to provide a structurally stable, flexible barrier that is relatively impermeable to most water-soluble substances. However, cells must obtain water-soluble nutrients, such as glucose and amino acids, from the environment. In addition, cells need to eliminate water-soluble waste products such as urea. These problems are overcome by special proteins scattered in the lipid bilayer. In fact, proteins make up about half of a membrane by weight, and they are responsible for many of the specialized functions of membranes.

Membrane Proteins

There are two distinct populations of membrane proteins: **integral proteins** and **peripheral proteins**. Integral proteins are inserted into the lipid bilayer; most are *transmembrane*, meaning that they span the entire width of the membrane, protruding on both sides. Integral proteins are mainly involved with transport functions (described below). In contrast, peripheral proteins are attached on either the inner or the outer surface of the membrane. These proteins often serve as enzymes or in mechanical functions, such as changing cell shape during cell division. The current view of the structure of biological membranes is called the **fluid-mosaic model** because the lipid portion has fluid properties, and the proteins dispersed within it form a mosaic pattern.

Many proteins on the extracellular side of membranes have attached sugar residues and are described as **glycoproteins**. The **glycocalyx** is the fuzzy, carbohydrate-rich area on cell surfaces. The glycocalyx is significant because it provides highly specific biological markers that can be recognized by other cells. For example, white blood cells of the immune system distinguish "self" cells of the body from invading bacterial cells by binding to certain membrane glycoproteins. In addition, sperm recognize an ovum by the egg's unique glycocalyx. The glycocalyx on red blood cells is what determines blood type. Unfortunately, continuous changes in the glycocalyx occur when cells become cancerous, often allowing these cells to evade attack and avoid destruction by the immune system.

Functions of Membrane Proteins

Membrane proteins serve a variety of important functions, giving cell membranes properties that otherwise would not be possible. Most notably, transmembrane proteins mediate the movement of substances into and out of cells (described in further detail in the next section). Membrane proteins also serve as enzymes, molecules that increase the rate of chemical reactions. In addition, membrane proteins exposed to the outside surface of cells may act as **receptors**. A receptor is a molecule with a specific binding site that fits the shape of a particular chemical messenger such as a hormone. In this way, chemical messages released by one cell type can communicate with another cell type, thereby influencing its activity. In a similar manner, some glycoproteins on the outer cell surface serve as identification tags that are specifically recognized by other cell proteins in a process called **cell-cell recognition**.

In addition, membrane proteins of adjacent cells may be linked together. These **cell adhesion molecules** (CAMs) provide temporary binding sites that guide cell migration. They may also provide more permanent attachments between cells. Unfortunately, CAMs often are not expressed in cancer cells. This explains why cells from a **tumor** may separate and spread to other locations in the body, a process known as **metastasis**. Finally, some membrane proteins provide attachment sites for the **cytoskeleton** and the **extracellular matrix** (nonliving material secreted by cells). These membrane proteins are important

WHY LARGE ORGANISMS CANNOT SURVIVE BY DIFFUSION ALONE

In the course of diffusion, individual molecules travel at relatively high velocities. For example, thermal motion of water molecules at body temperature is approximately 1,500 miles per hour (about 2,500 kilometers per hour). Surprisingly, however, the rate of movement from one location to another by diffusion is actually slow for distances much greater than about the size of a cell. This is because individual molecules cannot travel very far before they bump into another molecule. In water, for instance, a collision takes place about every 0.3 nanometers, and the constant bumping of molecules alters their direction of movement with each collision. Therefore, although individual molecules travel at high velocities, the number of collisions they undergo prevents them from traveling very far in a straight line. Consequently, diffusion can distribute molecules rapidly over very short distances (within the cytoplasm or between a few layers of cells), but the process is extremely slow over distances greater than a few centimeters.

As an illustration of the above concept, spray a small amount of perfume in the front of a room and time how long it takes for people in the back of the room to smell it. It will likely be within a for maintaining cell shape. They also help anchor and thereby fix the location of certain proteins within the fluid membrane.

DIFFUSION

Diffusion is the process by which particles spread spontaneously from regions where they are in higher concentration toward regions where they are in lower concentration. All atoms and molecules have **kinetic energy** as a result of heat in their environment. Consequently, they are in constant motion. As they move about randomly at relatively high speeds, they collide and ricochet off one another, changing direction with each collision (that is why diffusion is referred to as *random*

few minutes. Was that spread of perfume to the back of the room due to diffusion? Based on what you know about this process, your answer should be no. In fact, depending on the size of the room, it would likely take 15 to 20 days for molecules of perfume to reach the back by diffusion alone. So, how is it that people can smell the perfume after only a few minutes? The answer is that perfume molecules are carried by wind currents in a process known as *bulk flow*.

Based on what you know about diffusion, what can you predict about the distance between body tissues and nearby capillaries? Hint: If a capillary and a muscle cell were separated by 4 inches (about 10 centimeters, or cm), it would take over 11 years for glucose to diffuse that distance! Obviously, the distance is much less than that, which helps explain why capillaries are within diffusing distance of virtually every cell in your body.

As a general rule, diffusion is an efficient way to move substances across cell membranes. In fact, diffusion is the mechanism by which oxygen molecules cross lung tissue to enter the bloodstream and how oxygen leaves capillaries to enter body tissues. In contrast, bulk flow mechanisms are necessary to carry substances from one part of the body to another. For example, bulk flow is how air is brought into the lungs from the atmosphere when we inhale.

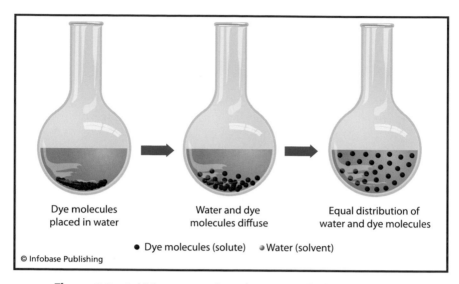

Dye molecules   Water and dye   Equal distribution of
placed in water   molecules diffuse   water and dye molecules

● Dye molecules (solute)   ● Water (solvent)

© Infobase Publishing

Figure 2.2   A high concentration of a water-soluble substance will eventually become equally distributed throughout a solution by diffusion. Diffusion is a process whereby random thermal motion distributes particles from regions where they are in higher concentration to regions where they are in lower concentration until they are equally distributed throughout the solution (equilibrium). At equilibrium, the molecules are still moving, but at equal rates in all directions.

thermal motion and why diffusion would cease at absolute zero, -273°C).

The overall effect of random thermal motion is that particles move away from areas of higher concentration, where collisions are more frequent, to areas of lower concentration (Figure 2.2). In this manner, particles are said to diffuse "down" their **concentration gradient**. In a closed system, diffusion will eventually produce a uniform distribution of particles, which is called a state of **equilibrium**. Although particles continue to move and collide after equilibrium is achieved, their concentration gradients no longer change because the particles move equally in all directions.

CONNECTIONS

The plasma membrane is an actively functioning part of living cells. In addition to maintaining cell integrity, it also controls the passage of materials into and out of the cell. Most organelles are also surrounded by a membrane. All cell membranes are composed of a phospholipid bilayer, with protein and cholesterol molecules dispersed within the layers. Membrane proteins serve a variety of diverse functions. For instance, they transport substances into and out of cells and also serve as cell-cell recognition sites. In addition, membrane proteins may act as enzymes, receptors, and cell adhesion molecules.

Diffusion is the process by which particles spread spontaneously from regions where they are in higher concentration to regions where they are in lower concentration. In this manner, particles are said to diffuse "down" their concentration gradient. Although individual molecules travel at high velocities, the number of collisions they undergo prevents them from traveling very far in a straight line. Consequently, diffusion can distribute molecules rapidly over short distances (within the cytoplasm or between a few layers of cells), but it is extremely slow over distances greater than a few centimeters.

3

Movement Through Cell Membranes

THE MOVEMENT OF MANY SUBSTANCES THROUGH CELL membranes involves **passive transport**; that is, processes such as simple diffusion, facilitated diffusion, osmosis, and filtration that do not require the expenditure of cell energy. In contrast, **active transport** processes, such as solute pumps, endocytosis, and exocytosis, require the expenditure of cell energy in the form of **adenosine triphosphate (ATP)**.

PASSIVE TRANSPORT MECHANISMS

The unassisted diffusion of lipid-soluble solutes through the plasma membrane is an example of simple diffusion. Such substances include oxygen, carbon dioxide, fat-soluble vitamins, and alcohol. These nonpolar substances are capable of passing through the hydrophobic interior of the plasma membrane. Their direction of net flow depends on the concentration gradient. For example, the concentration of oxygen molecules is always higher in the blood than in cells, so it continuously enters cells by simple diffusion. The opposite is true for carbon dioxide (Figure 3.1).

Most water-soluble substances, such as ions, cannot diffuse through the lipid portion of the cell membrane. In this case,

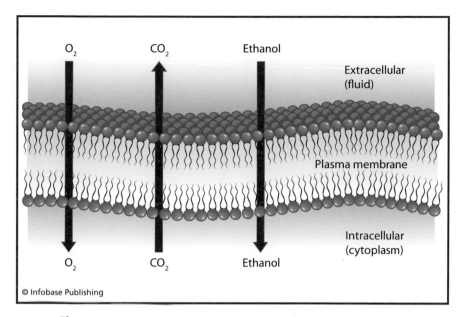

Figure 3.1 The cell membrane is selectively permeable, meaning that some substances can pass through it and some cannot. Fat-soluble substances, such as oxygen, carbon dioxide, and alcohol, pass through cell membranes by simple diffusion because they can dissolve in the lipid bilayer.

the substances diffuse through **channels**, which are special transmembrane proteins shaped like hollow cylinders. Because these proteins are filled with water, they create an aqueous pore that traverses the entire thickness of the membrane. Like a tunnel through a mountain, channels provide a pathway for small polar particles to diffuse through the membrane. Movement through channels is passive because it does not require energy from cells, and the direction of flow depends on the concentration gradient for the diffusing particle (Figure 3.2).

Under most circumstances, it would not be useful for a channel to be open all the time. For this reason, channels are "gated," which means they have the ability to open and close in response to an appropriate chemical or electrical signal. Channel pores also allow the passage of only certain substances.

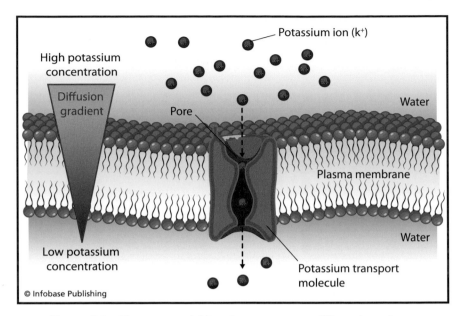

Figure 3.2 Most water-soluble substances cannot diffuse through a lipid bilayer. However, small polar or charged particles, such as water and ions, can cross a cell membrane by diffusing through protein structures called *channels*. The channels are water-filled pores that traverse the width of a membrane. This figure shows potassium ions diffusing through a potassium-permeable channel.

Most channels are primarily permeable to a specific inorganic ion such as sodium, potassium, calcium, or chloride.

Certain molecules, such as glucose, amino acids, and urea, are too polar to dissolve in the lipid bilayer and too large to pass through ion channels. However, they can move rapidly through the plasma membrane. This is accomplished by a passive process called **facilitated diffusion** in which the transported substance moves across the membrane by interacting with a protein **carrier** molecule. Although movement by facilitated diffusion follows a concentration gradient, the carrier is needed as a transport vehicle to allow a substance to cross the lipid bilayer. If you think of an ion channel as a passage with a gate, then a carrier protein could be loosely thought of as a revolving door. In other words, unlike the channel, which has a continuous tunnel traversing a membrane, a carrier appears to have a binding site that is moved from one face of the membrane to the other by conformational changes in the protein. In addition, as with channels, carriers tend to be highly selective as to what they will transport.

Osmosis is a special case of diffusion. Osmosis is the diffusion of water molecules from a region of higher water concentration (lower solute concentration) to a region of lower water concentration (higher solute concentration) across a selectively permeable membrane (Figure 3.3). In solutions, solute particles take up space that water molecules would otherwise occupy. Thus, a higher concentration of solute means a lower concentration of water. The extent to which the water concentration is decreased by solute particles depends only on their number and not their size, kind, or charge. For example, if there is distilled water on both sides of a selectively permeable membrane, no net flow of water (osmosis) occurs. However, if the solute concentration on the two sides of a membrane differs, the water concentration also differs, and water then diffuses across the membrane from the region of lower solute concentration (higher water concentration) to the region of higher solute concentration (lower water concentration).

The flow of water across a membrane by osmosis can change the volumes on both sides of the membrane. Consequently, the movement of water into a closed system, such as a cell, will exert pressure against the plasma membrane, which is referred to as **osmotic pressure**. Osmotic imbalances (differences in the total solute concentration on the two sides of a membrane) cause cells to swell or shrink due to net water gain or loss. The cells change size until they reach equilibrium; that is, until the water concentration is the same on both sides of the plasma membrane. Alternatively, before equilibrium is reached, the cell could swell to the point of bursting. The concentration of water and solutes everywhere inside the body must therefore be regulated so it is the same on both sides of cell membranes. This keeps cells from changing their volume.

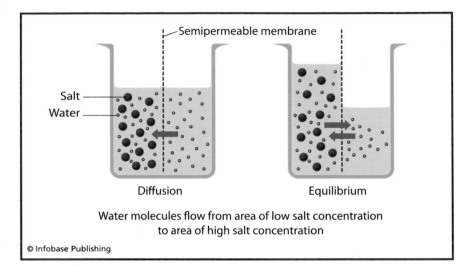

Figure 3.3   In this system, the membrane separating these two solutions is permeable to water but not to solute (salt). As a consequence, water moves by osmosis from the compartment containing a lower solute concentration—a higher water concentration (right side)—to the solution with a higher solute concentration—lower water concentration (left side)—until equilibrium is reached. Note that as a result of water flow across the membrane, the volume of the right compartment decreased.

Solutions that have the same solute concentrations as cells and body fluids are said to be isotonic, and they do not cause cells to change size. In contrast, a solution with a higher solute concentration than body fluids is **hypertonic**. Cells placed in a hypertonic medium will shrink due to the net movement of water out of the cell. On the other hand, cells exposed to a hypotonic solution, which has a lower solute concentration than body fluids, will gain water by osmosis and swell. In fact, under some hypotonic conditions, cells swell to the point of breaking, analogous to a balloon that is overinflated with air (Figure 3.4).

Water can move quite rapidly through cell membranes via protein channels called **aquaporins**. The number of aquaporins in some kidney cells is under hormonal control (antidiuretic

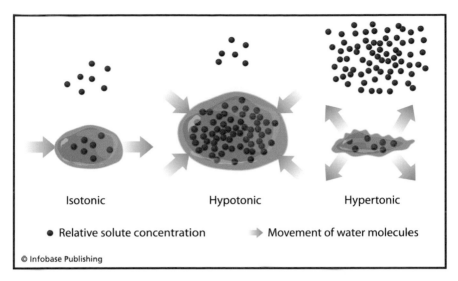

Isotonic   Hypotonic   Hypertonic

● Relative solute concentration   ➡ Movement of water molecules

© Infobase Publishing

Figure 3.4   The effect of solutions of different salt concentrations on living cells. Isotonic solutions have the same solute concentration as the cell interior so that the cells retain their normal size and shape. Cells placed in a hypotonic solution gain water and swell because the concentration of solutes in hypotonic solutions is less than in cells, which generates a driving force for water to flow into cells by osmosis. In contrast, cells placed in hypertonic solutions tend to shrink from loss of water.

hormone released from the pituitary gland), which is important for regulating how much fluid is eliminated from the body in urine. In some instances, water and solute particles are forced through membranes by **hydrostatic pressure** by a process called **filtration**. The force for this movement usually comes from blood pressure, which is created largely by the pumping action of the heart. Like diffusion, filtration across a membrane is a passive process. However, in this case the driving force is a pressure gradient that actually pushes solute-containing fluid from the higher-pressure area to a lower-pressure area. For example, filtration of blood by the kidneys is the first step in urine formation, whereby kidney tubules collect fluid and solutes. Amazingly, every day your kidneys filter approximately

48 gallons (about 180 liters, or L) of blood, which means your entire blood volume is filtered about 35 times each day.

ACTIVE TRANSPORT MECHANISMS

Sometimes particles move across cell membranes against their concentration gradients; that is, from a region of lower concentration to one of higher concentration. This type of movement is called active transport, and it requires cells to use energy from the breakdown of ATP to ADP. Substances moved across a membrane in this manner are usually unable to pass in the necessary direction by any of the passive processes. For example, they may be too large to traverse channels and carriers, they may not dissolve in the lipid bilayer, or they may have to move "uphill" against their concentration gradients. It is estimated that up to 40% of a cell's energy supply (ATP) is used for active transport through membranes. There are two major mechanisms of transport that require ATP: solute pumping and vesicular transport.

Solute pumping is similar to facilitated diffusion in that it involves specific carrier molecules in the cell membrane. These protein molecules have binding sites that combine temporarily and specifically with the particles to be transported. However, whereas facilitated diffusion is driven by the kinetic energy of the diffusing particles, solute pumps require ATP produced by cells. Because this type of transport moves substances against their concentration gradients, the carrier proteins are referred to as *pumps*.

The most common active transport carrier is the *sodium-potassium pump*. This protein simultaneously transports sodium ions out of the cell and potassium ions into the cell. Consequently, it keeps intracellular sodium levels low, while also keeping intracellular levels of potassium relatively high (about 20 to 30 times greater than that in the extracellular fluid). The artificial concentration gradients maintained by the pump are necessary for nerve and muscle cells to function normally, and also for body cells to maintain their normal fluid volumes. Because of the concentration gradients, there is a continual leakage of sodium ions into the cell and potassium ions out of the cell; therefore, this pump operates more or less continuously. The pump can also change its rate of transport, depending on the level of sodium and potassium movement. For example, the pump activity temporarily increases during nerve impulses or muscle contraction when there is a transient increase in membrane permeability for sodium and potassium ions. Another example of active transport occurs in stomach cells, where a potassium-hydrogen pump functions in the formation of hydrochloric acid.

Some substances that cannot move across the plasma membrane by any other means are transported by **vesicular transport**. Endocytosis ("into the cell") describes vesicular transport where particles are brought into a cell after they are engulfed or enclosed within small, membrane-bound sacs, or **vesicles** (Figure 3.5a). Once a vesicle is formed, it detaches from the plasma membrane and moves into the cytoplasm, where it often fuses with a cellular organelle that contains digestive enzymes. This mechanism is well suited for the transport of relatively large particles such as bacteria or dead body cells. In **phagocytosis**, which literally means "cell eating," a cell engulfs

YOUR HEALTH: REGARDING OSMOSIS

Osmosis is an important consideration when health-care providers give intravenous solutions to patients. For example, if a treatment is designed to infuse patients with solutions that have the same solute and water concentration as body cells, then an **isotonic solution** would need to be used. However, sometimes **hypertonic solutions** are given to patients who have swollen feet and hands due to fluid retention. Such solutions draw water out of the tissue spaces into the bloodstream so it can be eliminated by the kidneys. In contrast, hypotonic solutions may be infused to rehydrate tissues of extremely dehydrated patients.

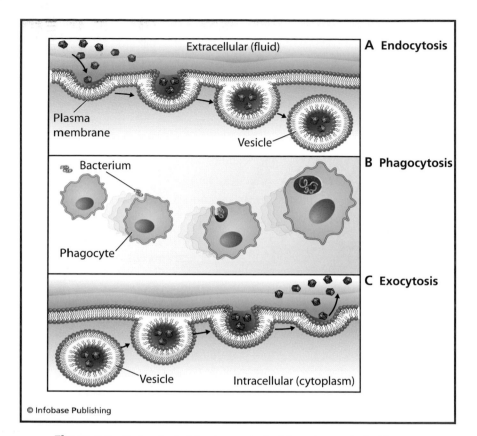

Figure 3.5 Endocytosis (a), phagocytosis (b), and exocytosis (c) are processes for moving substances into and out of cells. In endocytosis and phagocytosis, the cell membrane surrounds the particles and closes around them, drawing the particles into the cell. Phagocytosis is used primarily by white blood cells to engulf and destroy bacteria, viruses, or other large foreign particles that could cause harm to the body. Exocytosis is the reverse endocytosis. The particles, contained within a vesicle, move to the edge of the cell where the vesicle fuses with the cell membrane and releases the particles to the outside of the cell.

a particle, which is enclosed in a vesicle within the cell (Figure 3.5b). Phagocytosis is routinely conducted by a type of white blood cell called a *phagocyte*. On the other hand, **pinocytosis**, or "cell drinking," is commonly used by cells to take in liquids that contain dissolved proteins or fats. Pinocytosis is like phagocytosis except that only liquid is engulfed by the cell.

YOUR HEALTH: CYSTIC FIBROSIS

Mutations that affect channel selectively or their regulation can have serious health consequences. For example, cystic fibrosis, the most common inherited disorder among Caucasians, results from a malfunctioning chloride channel, which causes abnormal secretion in **exocrine glands**. As a result, this disease causes the respiratory tract to fill with abnormally thick mucus, and also prevents the pancreas from properly producing digestive enzymes. Defective ion channels also are responsible for diseases that lead to improper rhythm of the heart, high blood pressure, low blood sugar from excessive insulin secretion, and several neurological disorders. In fact, epilepsy, migraine headaches, and certain forms of deafness all are neurological disorders that can be caused by mutations in genes for ion channels.

Exocytosis ("out of the cell") refers to vesicular transport in which particles are eliminated from cells (Figure 3.5c). Products to be secreted are first enclosed in small vesicles. The vesicles migrate to the plasma membrane and fuse with it. This mechanism is often used to secrete hormones (for example, insulin), mucus, and other cell products, or to eject certain cellular wastes.

CONNECTIONS

Many substances move across membrane surfaces by passive transport, a process that does not require cellular energy. Passive transport processes include simple diffusion, facilitated diffusion, osmosis, and filtration. In contrast, active transport mechanisms, such as the movement of solutes by using pumps or by endocytosis and exocytosis, require cellular energy in the form of ATP.

(continues)

(continued)

Osmosis is a special case of diffusion that occurs when water molecules diffuse from a region of higher water concentration to a region of lower water concentration across a selectively permeable membrane. Solutions that have the same osmotic pressure as cells and body fluids are isotonic and do not cause a net flow of water or a change in cell size. In contrast, a solution with a higher osmotic pressure (a higher solute concentration) than body fluids is hypertonic, and cells placed in this environment will shrink due to the net movement of water out of the cell. Cells exposed to a hypotonic solution, which has a lower osmotic pressure (a lower solute concentration) than body fluids, will gain water by osmosis and swell.

4

Cell Cytoplasm

THE MATERIAL THAT FILLS THE CELL BETWEEN ITS PLASMA membrane and its nucleus is called the cytoplasm. Most cellular activities take place in the cytoplasm. In a sense, it could be thought of as a "manufacturing" area of a cell. Not surprisingly, early scientists using light microscopes thought the cytoplasm was essentially a structureless and functionless gel because it is essentially a clear, colorless substance. However, electron microscopes, which provide much greater magnification and resolution, revealed that the cytoplasm is filled with a rich network of membranes and structures. In fact, the cytoplasm consists of three major components: the cytosol, organelles, and **inclusions**.

COMPONENTS OF THE CYTOPLASM

The cytosol is a semitransparent, viscous (thick) fluid in which all the other cytoplasmic elements are suspended. The cytosol is mainly composed of water with nutrients and other solutes dissolved in it.

Inclusions are chemical substances that may or may not be present, depending on the cell type. Most inclusions are stored nutrients or cell products. For instance, fat droplets in adipose cells and glycogen granules in liver cells are both examples of inclusions that are energy storage compounds. (Fat is for long-term energy storage whereas glycogen, a polymer of glucose, is a readily available source of energy.) Mucus and pigments, such as **melanin** in skin and hair cells, are inclusions that contain cell products.

Organelles ("little organs") are the structures that actually carry out particular functions for the cell as a whole. Loosely speaking, they are analogous to organs, which carry out complex and specific functions for the entire organism. Some organelles, such as the cytoskeleton, ribosomes, and centrioles, lack membranes, but most organelles are surrounded by membranes that are similar in composition and function to the plasma membrane. These membranous organelles include the mitochondria, endoplasmic reticulum, Golgi apparatus, lysosomes, and peroxisomes.

Ribosomes

Ribosomes are tiny, round, nonmembranous structures made of proteins and RNA. They are the actual sites of protein synthesis within cells, At the ribosomes, amino acids, the building blocks of proteins, are linked together to form polypeptides. Interestingly, the ribosomes of prokaryotic cells have a different structure than those found in eukaryotic cells. In fact, scientists have exploited this difference with antibiotics that are specific to prokaryotic ribosomes. These antibiotics block protein synthesis in bacterial cells while leaving eukaryotic cells intact.

Ribosomes are found both loose in the cytoplasm and attached to the surface of an organelle called the endoplasmic reticulum (Figure 4.1). The free ribosomes produce soluble proteins that function within the cytosol. Proteins synthesized by the attached ribosomes are secreted from the cell or incorporated into cell membranes.

Endoplasmic Reticulum

The cytomembrane system refers to a series of organelles (endoplasmic reticulum, Golgi apparatus, and vesicles) that synthesize lipids and also modify new polypeptide chains into complete functional proteins. This system also sorts and ships its products to different locations within the cell.

The cytomembrane system begins with the **endoplasmic reticulum (ER)**, a complex organelle composed of flattened membranous sacs and elongated canals that twist through the cytoplasm (Figure 4.1). In fact, the ER accounts for about half of the total membrane of a cell. The ER is continuous with the membrane that surrounds the nucleus, and it also interconnects and communicates with other organelles. In this capacity, it serves as a micro "circulatory system" for the cell by providing a network of channels that carry substances from one region to another. There are two distinct types of ER: rough ER and smooth ER. The rough ER has many ribosomes attached to its outer surface. This gives it a studded appearance when viewed with an electron microscope. In contrast, the smooth ER lacks ribosomes.

Rough ER has several functions. Its ribosomes synthesize all the proteins secreted from cells. Consequently, rough ER is especially abundant in cells that export proteins, such as the white blood cells that make antibodies and the pancreatic cells that produce digestive enzymes. The newly synthesized polypeptides move directly from the ribosomes into ER tubules, where they are further processed and modified. For example, sugar groups may be added to form glycoproteins. In addition, proteins typically fold into complex, three-dimensional shapes. The rough ER then encloses the newly synthesized proteins into vesicles, which pinch off and travel to the Golgi apparatus. The rough ER is also responsible for forming the constituents of cell membranes, such as integral proteins and phospholipids.

Smooth ER is continuous with rough ER, but it does not synthesize proteins. Instead, it produces certain lipid molecules such as the steroid hormones testosterone and estrogen. Smooth ER also functions in the detoxification of some metabolic products, drugs, and alcohol. Because the liver is important for handling toxins, its cells have a well-developed, smooth ER. Skeletal muscle cells also have a large amount of smooth ER

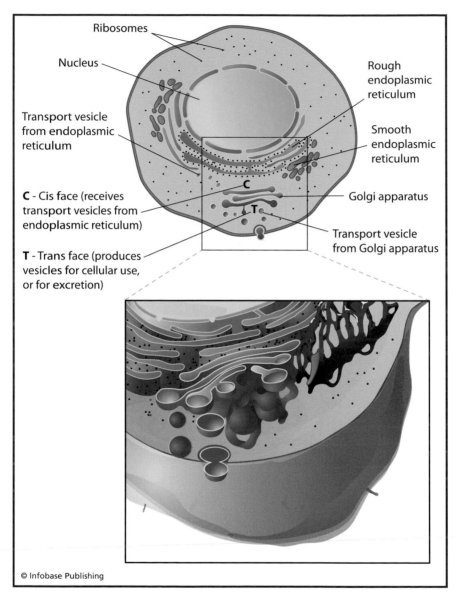

Ribosomes

Nucleus

Rough endoplasmic reticulum

Transport vesicle from endoplasmic reticulum

Smooth endoplasmic reticulum

C - Cis face (receives transport vesicles from endoplasmic reticulum)

Golgi apparatus

Transport vesicle from Golgi apparatus

T - Trans face (produces vesicles for cellular use, or for excretion)

© Infobase Publishing

Figure 4.1   The Golgi apparatus receives proteins from the endoplasmic reticulum, adds any necessary finishing touches, and prepares the proteins for delivery to various parts of the cell.

that is specifically modified to store calcium ions. The release of this calcium, which is stimulated by appropriate nerve activity, is necessary for muscle contraction.

Golgi Apparatus

The **Golgi apparatus** appears as stacks of flattened membranous sacs (Figure 4.1). Whereas the ER synthesizes the products, the Golgi processes and transports them. Its enzymes put the finishing touches on newly synthesized proteins and lipids arriving from the rough ER. For example, sugar groups may be added or removed, and phosphate groups may also be attached. The Golgi apparatus then sorts out various products and packages them in vesicles for transport to specific locations. Thus, like an assembly line, vesicles from the ER fuse with the Golgi apparatus on one side, and newly formed transport vesicles containing the finished product bud off the opposite side. Some of these vesicles may fuse with the plasma membrane for subsequent exocytosis of product. Alternatively, they may fuse with various organelles in the cytoplasm.

Vesicles

Vesicles are tiny, membranous sacs found in the cytoplasm. **Lysosomes** are vesicular organelles that bud from Golgi membranes. They contain powerful digestive enzymes that break down nutrient molecules and foreign particles. For instance, phagocytic white blood cells, such as *macrophages*, engulf bacteria, which are then digested by lysosomal enzymes. Lysosomes are also used to destroy worn-out cell parts. In this way, they can be thought of as the garbage disposal system for cells.

Peroxisomes are tiny, membrane-bound sacs that function in the breakdown of fatty acids and amino acids. They also detoxify a number of poisonous substances. However, the most important function of peroxisomes is the removal of **free radicals**, highly reactive chemicals, such as O_2, that are normally produced during cell metabolism. Cigarette smoke and ultraviolet radiation create additional free radicals. Because free radicals contain unpaired electrons, they have a powerful ability to react with other molecules, thereby interfering with their proper function. Oxidation refers to the process by which an atom or molecule loses one or more electrons to another atom or molecule (such as to a free radical), which can disrupt both its structure and ability to function. Oxidation, for instance, is what causes metal to rust. Consequently, an excess of free radicals can alter essential molecules, such as DNA and enzymes (proteins), thereby affecting overall health. In fact, excess free radicals have been implicated with cardiovascular disease, aging, and Alzheimer's disease. An antioxidant is a chemical that gives up an electron to a free radical before the radical has a chance to damage some other molecule. The body produces some natural antioxidants, including the hormone melatonin,

YOUR HEALTH: LYSOSOMES

There are several diseases associated with malfunctioning lysosomes. For example, this organelle does not function properly in people with Tay-Sachs disease, an inherited disorder that is most prevalent in Ashkenazi (central European) Jewish children. Those afflicted with this disease lack a single lysosomal enzyme (out of about 40). This, in turn, negatively affects brain cells where this enzyme is important for the continual degradation of certain glycolipids. As a result of this disease, undigested lipids accumulate in nerve cells, interfering with the proper functioning of the nervous system. Affected individuals usually show symptoms of listlessness and motor weakness by 3 to 6 months of age. Soon thereafter, mental retardation, seizures, and blindness occur. The disease ultimately leads to death, usually within a year and a half of birth.

Lysosome activity is also important for shrinking or removing particular tissues at certain times during development. For example, lysosome digestion is responsible for removing the webbing between fingers and toes in a human fetus. It is also responsible for degrading a tadpole's tail as the animal develops into an adult frog. In addition, lysosomal digestion of tissue occurs in the uterus after childbirth, in the breasts after weaning an infant, and in skeletal muscles during periods of prolonged inactivity.

which neutralizes some free radicals. In addition, carotenoids, the orange pigments found in carrots and pumpkins, and foods rich in vitamins C and E provide antioxidant activity. Presently, there is much debate concerning the health benefits and risks of supplementing the diet with antioxidant vitamins.

Mitochondria

Mitochondria are considered the "power plants" of cells because they produce most of its ATP (a small amount of ATP is produced in the cytoplasm). The metabolic processes that produce ATP in this organelle depend upon a continuous supply of oxygen. They also produce carbon dioxide as a by-product. Mitochondria are particularly abundant in metabolically active cells such as those in skeletal muscle and the liver.

Mitochondria are fluid-filled, slipper-shaped organelles that vary in size and shape. (Figure 4.2). Their outer boundaries consists of two separate cell membranes: a smooth outer membrane and an inner membrane that has a number of large infoldings called *cristae*, which increase the surface area. Some of the enzymes necessary to make ATP are physically part of the cristae (integral and peripheral membrane proteins). Other enzymes are dissolved in the fluid within the **matrix** (the region enclosed by the inner membrane). Cyanide gas is highly toxic because it blocks the production of ATP in mitochondria.

Cytoskeleton

Throughout the cell cytoplasm there is an elaborate network of protein structures called the cytoskeleton (Figure 4.3). These structures can be thought of as both the bones and muscles of cells, because they provide a physical framework that determines cell shape, reinforces the plasma membrane and **nuclear envelope**, and acts as scaffolds for membrane and cytoplasmic proteins; they are also involved in intracellular transport and various types of cell movements. Many of these elements of the cytoskeleton are permanent. However, some appear only at certain times in a **cell cycle**. For example,

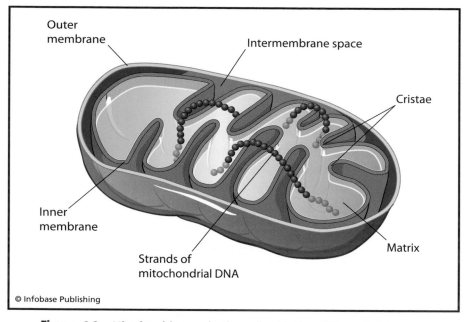

Outer membrane

Intermembrane space

Cristae

Inner membrane

Strands of mitochondrial DNA

Matrix

© Infobase Publishing

Figure 4.2 Mitochondria supply the cell with the ATP needed to perform its life activities. Mitochondria are surrounded by two separate membranes. The inner membrane has many folds, called cristae, which increase the surface area for ATP production. The matrix, enclosed by the inner membrane, is an enzyme-rich fluid.

before cell division, *spindle fibers* form; these structures act to separate the **chromosomes** and distribute them to each of the newly formed daughter cells. When cell division is complete, the spindle fibers disassemble. As might be expected, energy from ATP is needed for cytoskeletal movements.

The largest structures of the cytoskeleton are **microtubules**, long, hollow cylinders that help to determine overall cell shape. They also act like railroad tracks, allowing organelles to distribute various materials appropriately within the cytoplasm. In addition, microtubules are vital to cell division because they form the spindle fibers. *Colchicine*, a chemical produced by the autumn crocus (*Colchicum*), is a poison that blocks assembly and promotes disassembly of microtubules, affecting animals that eat these plants. This chemical is used

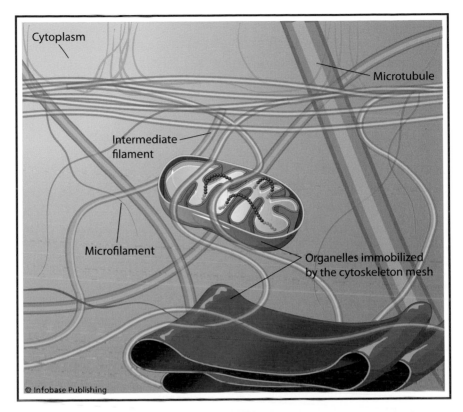

Figure 4.3 Elements of the cytoskeleton. Microfilaments are strands of the protein actin and are involved with cell motility and changes in cell shape. Intermediate filaments are tough protein fibers with a ropelike structure; they act as internal wires to resist pulling forces on the cell. Microtubules are hollow tubes made of the protein tubulin. They help determine overall cell shape and the distribution of cellular organelles.

by scientists to block cell division in order to study cell reproduction and cancer. Another plant product, taxol, is a poison from the western yew (*Taxus brevifolia*). It also blocks cell division by disrupting microtubules. Taxol was the basis of a successful drug that inhibits the growth of some tumors, including breast cancer.

The thinnest cytoskeletal elements are **microfilaments**, which are composed primarily of the protein *actin*. Microfilaments are involved with cell motility and in producing changes in cell shape. The most stable of the three cytoskeletal elements are the ropelike **intermediate filaments** that mechanically strengthen and help maintain the shape of cells and their parts. In some cases, they can be thought of as internal wires that resist pulling forces.

Centrioles, Cilia, and Flagella

Centrioles consist of two hollow, nonmembranous cylinders that lie at right angles to each other. They are primarily made of microtubules. Centrioles are important in cell reproduction, where they function with spindle fibers to distribute chromosomes. In some cells, centrioles also give rise to extensions called **cilia** and **flagella**. Cilia occur in precise patterns and rows on a cell surface, displaying coordinated beating

CELL COMPARTMENTS

Not only does the plasma membrane separate the cell interior from the environment, membranes make it possible for various organelles to maintain an internal environment different from that of the surrounding cytosol. In fact, this compartmentalization is absolutely crucial to cell functioning. For example, if all the chemicals in mitochondria were placed in a test tube, only a small number of the needed metabolic reactions would occur. This is because cell membranes are necessary for the constituents of an organelle to be appropriately separated or appropriately mixed in order to function as they do in the living cell. Further, membrane compartmentalization prevents the thousands of cellular enzymes and chemicals from randomly mixing, which would cause chaos. Peter Mitchell received a Nobel Prize in 1978 for his *chemiosmotic hypothesis*, which describes the role of mitochondrial membranes in the production of ATP, a process that depends on the compartmentalization of enzymatically driven reactions.

Figure 4.4 The movement of the cilia that line the respiratory tract help to prevent smoke and other foreign particles from entering the lungs. They can also help to propel an entire organism, as is the case with some protozoa, whose outer surface is covered with cilia.

patterns that produce a wave of motion that sweeps over their surface (Figure 4.4). Ciliated cells line the respiratory tract, where the movement of the cilia carry mucus and debris away from the lungs. This ciliary motion is temporarily paralyzed by cigarette smoke, which explains why regular smokers have a chronic cough. Flagella are considerably longer than cilia and display an undulating wavelike motion. The only flagellated cells found in humans are sperm cells.

DID YOU KNOW?

Mitochondria are unusual organelles. In terms of their size and biochemistry, they closely resemble bacteria. In fact, they have their own DNA and ribosomes. However, mitochondrial DNA is circular, like DNA found in bacteria. In addition, mitochondrial ribosomes are more similar to bacterial ribosomes than the ribosomes of eukaryotic cells. Further, the inner membrane of mitochondria closely resembles a bacterial plasma membrane. Taken altogether, the above evidence is used to support the theory of *endosymbiosis* (*endo* means "within" and *symbiosis* means "living together.") This theory proposes that over 1.2 billion years ago, some forms of free-living bacteria were engulfed by predatory, amoebalike cells, yet they escaped digestion. Over time, these ancient bacteria evolved into modern mitochondria and developed a permanent symbiotic relationship with their host cells.

Mitochondria also have the ability to divide on their own. This helps explain how their number may increase in cells undergoing higher levels of metabolic activity. For example, regular exercise will lead to an increase in the number of mitochondria in skeletal muscle. This, in turn, allows the cells of an athlete to produce more ATP than those of a sedentary person.

CONNECTIONS

The cellular material located outside the nucleus and inside the plasma membrane is called the cytoplasm. It is the site of most cellular activities. The cytoplasm consists of the cytosol, organelles, and inclusions.

Ribosomes are tiny, round, nonmembranous structures made of proteins and RNA. They are the sites of protein synthesis. The endoplasmic reticulum (ER) is a complex organelle composed of flattened membranous sacs and elongated canals that twist through the cytoplasm. Rough ER has many ribosomes attached to its outer surface; the ribosomes synthesize proteins that are secreted from the cell. Rough ER also forms constituents of cell membranes, such as integral proteins and phospholipids.

Smooth ER lacks ribosomes; it is the site of synthesis of certain lipid molecules, and it detoxifies some metabolic toxins. The Golgi apparatus puts the finishing touches on newly synthesized proteins and lipids that are arriving from the rough ER. It also packages them in vesicles for transport to specific locations.

Lysosomes are organelles that contain powerful digestive enzymes used to break down nutrients and foreign particles. Peroxisomes are tiny, membrane-bound sacs that detoxify a number of poisonous substances and are important in the removal of free radicals. Mitochondria are double-membraned organelles that produce most of a cell's ATP.

The cytoskeleton, an elaborate network of protein structures in the cytoplasm, consists of microtubules, microfilaments, and intermediate filaments. These tubules and filaments provide a physical framework that determines cell shape, reinforces the plasma membrane and nuclear envelope, and acts as scaffolds for membrane and cytoplasmic proteins. They are also involved in intracellular transport and cell movements.

5

The Nucleus: The Command Center of the Cell

THE NUCLEUS OF A CELL IS A SPHERICAL OR OVAL STRUCTURE averaging about 0.0002 inches (about 5 μm) in diameter, making it the largest cytoplasmic organelle. It is usually located near the center of a cell and is surrounded by a double-layered nuclear envelope, consisting of inner and outer lipid bilayers. The nucleus is considered the "command center" of a cell. Its DNA contains the genetic code that has the instructions to produce virtually every protein in the body (recall that mitochondria have their own DNA and produce some proteins not coded for in nuclear DNA). In addition, the nucleus also directs the kinds and amounts of proteins that are synthesized at any given time.

The nucleus has three distinct constituents: the nuclear envelope, the **nucleolus** (plural: **nucleoli**), and **chromatin**. These structures are discussed below.

NUCLEAR ENVELOPE

Like mitochondria, the nucleus is bound by a double membrane barrier called the **nuclear envelope**. It consists of two lipid bilayers in which numerous protein molecules are embedded. Within the nuclear envelope is the **nucleoplasm**, the fluid portion of the nucleus. Like the cytoplasm, nucleoplasm contains dissolved salts and nutrients. The outer layer of the nuclear envelope is continuous with rough ER and is also studded with numerous ribosomes. The inner surface has attachment sites for protein filaments that maintain the shape of the nucleus and also anchor DNA molecules, helping to keep them organized.

The nuclear envelope keeps water-soluble substances from moving freely into and out of the nucleus. However, at various points, the two layers of membrane fuse together. **Nuclear pores**, composed of clusters of proteins, are found at such regions and span the full thickness of both layers of the nuclear envelope. The pores allow the passage of ions and small, water-soluble substances; they also regulate entry and exit of large particles, such as ribosomal subunits (Figure 5.1).

NUCLEOLI

Each nucleus contains one or more nucleoli ("little nuclei"), small, nonmembranous, dense bodies composed largely of RNA and protein. Nucleoli are the sites of assembly of ribosomal subunits. Accordingly, they are associated with specific

RED BLOOD CELL NUCLEUS

Every type of cell in the body contains a nucleus except for mature red blood cells. Red blood cells in the process of forming have nuclei, but the nuclei are lost before these cells leave the bone marrow and enter the bloodstream. As a consequence, these **anucleate** mature cells cannot synthesize proteins. Therefore, circulating red blood cells do not have the ability to replace enzymes or structural parts that break down. For this reason, they have a limited life span of approximately three to four months. In contrast, some other cell types contain many nuclei, such as those in skeletal muscle and the liver. The presence of multiple nuclei usually indicates a relatively large mass of cytoplasm that must be regulated.

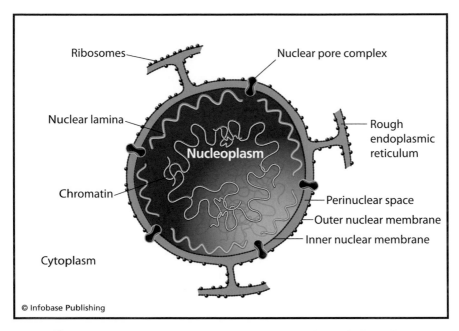

Figure 5.1   A diagrammatic view of the nuclear envelope, which consists of a double membrane with pores. The two membranes are separated by a perinuclear space. The outer nuclear membrane is continuous with the rough ER of the cytoplasm. The inner membrane is lined with a network of protein filaments, the nuclear lamina, that maintain the shape of the nucleus. The nuclear pores consist of a complex of proteins that regulate entry and exit of large particles. The nuclear envelope encloses a gel-like fluid called the nucleoplasm in which other elements are suspended. Chromatin is composed of approximately equal amounts of DNA and histone proteins, which provide a physical means for packing the very long DNA molecules into a limited space.

regions of chromatin, the chromosomal material that contains the DNA needed for synthesizing ribosomal RNA. Once ribosomal subunits are formed, they migrate to the cytoplasm through nuclear pores.

CHROMATIN

Chromatin consists of loosely coiled fibers of DNA and *histone proteins* (Figure 5.2). The DNA contains the information for synthesis of specific proteins. A segment of DNA that

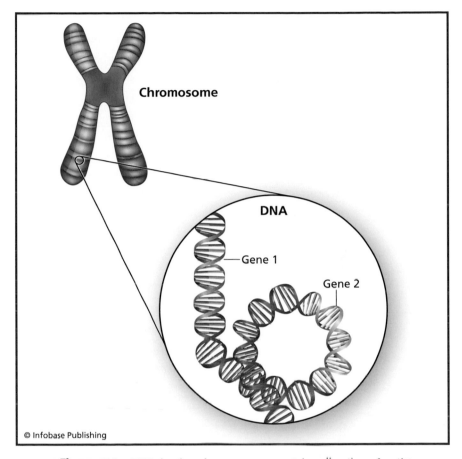

Figure 5.2 DNA in the chromosomes contains directions for the synthesis of nearly all the proteins in the body. A gene is a portion of the DNA that contains information for the synthesis of one polypeptide or protein. It is estimated that humans have approximately 35,000 different genes, which control all aspects of human life from hair color to predispostion to certain diseases.

codes for a specific protein is a gene. It is estimated humans have around 35,000 different genes. The histone protein molecules associated with chromatin help package a great deal of DNA into a small space. To fully appreciate this task, keep in mind that a nucleus is only about 0.0002 inches (5 μm) in diameter. However, the total length of DNA in each nucleus is around 2 inches (5 cm). Thus, packing the DNA into a nucleus requires nearly a 10,000-fold reduction in length! This is accomplished by wrapping DNA around clusters of histone proteins, forming structures called *nucleosomes* that look like beads on a string. In addition, other proteins associated with chromatin help regulate which genes are active.

When a somatic cell is preparing to divide, it duplicates its DNA molecules so each daughter cell will receive a complete, exact copy of the hereditary instructions. In addition, prior to cell division, chromatin is folded and twisted into condensed structures called chromosomes. Chromosomes greatly compact the already condensed genetic material in chromatin, preventing entanglement and breakage of the delicate strands during cell division movement.

CELL AGING

Aging of individual cells is responsible for many of the problems associated with old age of an organism. Cell aging is a complicated phenomenon that is not completely understood. Some researchers suggest that it results from continual small challenges from toxins, which over time lead to permanent cell damage. For instance, pesticides, alcohol, certain environmental pollutants, and bacterial toxins may damage cell membranes, change the activity of enzymes, and cause mistakes in DNA structure (mutations). In addition, free radicals produced by mitochondria during normal metabolism may damage organelles, which in turn weakens and ages a cell. Free radicals also are generated by exposure to radiation such as ultraviolet light and X-rays.

Other researchers have found that aging also causes a progressive weakening of the immune system. As a result, the body becomes less able to fight damaging infections. In addition, with age, the immune system becomes more likely to attack its own body tissues (*autoimmunity*), leading to their destruction.

Some molecular biologists suggest aging is programmed in the genes. Their evidence comes from the study of **telomeres**, special caps on the end of chromosomes that protect them from fraying or fusing with other chromosomes (by loose analogy, telomeres function similarly as aglets on the end of shoelaces). Telomeres may be related to aging because they shorten slightly after each cell division, and when they reach a certain minimal length, cells stop dividing and die. For instance, cells taken from a newborn child can divide in culture over 100 times, whereas cells from an octogenarian may only divide a couple of dozen times before they stop dividing and die. With this in mind, some searching for a "fountain of youth" suggest the use of chemicals that prevent telomere loss, which in turn may prolong life.

THE CELL CYCLE

The cell cycle refers to the series of changes that a cell undergoes from the time it forms until it reproduces. The stages of the cell cycle include interphase, mitosis, cytoplasmic division, and differentiation (Figure 5.3).

Interphase describes the period when a cell grows and undergoes its normal metabolic activities. It is usually the longest phase in the cell cycle. Toward the middle or end of interphase, the DNA *replicates* (makes an exact copy of itself) as the cell prepares for division.

Many kinds of body cells grow and reproduce, thereby increasing their number, as when a child grows into an adult. In addition, cell division is necessary to replace cells with short life spans, such as those that form skin or the lining of the stomach (which is replaced about every three to five days). Cell division also takes place during tissue repair.

Mitosis refers to division of the nucleus (Figure 5.4). It results in the formation of two daughter nuclei, both with exactly the same genes as the original cell. Although mitosis is described in terms of phases, it is actually a continuous process. Depending on the type of cell, it may take from five minutes to several hours to complete.

The first stage of mitosis, **prophase**, is characterized by condensation of chromatin into chromosomes. In addition,

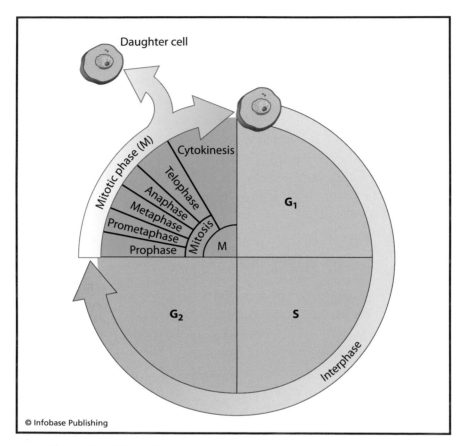

Figure 5.3 The cell cycle. A cell undergoes many changes from its formation until the time it reproduces. G_1 and G_2 are growth stages, during which the cell matures. The chromosomes replicate during the S (synthesis) stage. G_1, G_2, and S are all stages of interphase. During the M (mitotic) phase, the cell undergoes the five stages of mitosis (prophase, prometaphase, metaphase, anaphase, and telophase), as well as cytokinesis, where the two new daughter cells are formed.

the centrioles replicate, spindle fibers appear, and the nuclear envelope and nucleoli disappear. Once the nuclear envelope is gone, some of the spindle microtubules attach to chromosomes, throwing them into an agitated motion during late prophase, or prometaphase. **Metaphase** describes the stage during which the chromosomes line up on the *metaphase plate* located midway between the centrioles. This is followed by **anaphase**, during which the spindle fibers shorten and pull apart the *chromatids*, the two halves of the replicated chromosomes. The separated chromatids become individual chromosomes. Finally, in **telophase**, in both of the forming cells, the nuclear envelope and nucleoli reappear and the chromosomes unwind, forming threadlike chromatin.

Cytokinesis describes the events in the division of the cytoplasm. It usually begins during late anaphase, when the cell membrane starts to pinch in, and it is completed during telophase. Cytokinesis occurs due to contraction of a ring of microfilaments that form a **cleavage furrow** over the midline of the spindle, thereby pinching the original mass of cytoplasm into two parts (Figure 5.4g).

In each individual, all body cells originate from a single cell—the fertilized egg, or **zygote**, which is produced by the fusion of the egg and sperm. Sperm and eggs, the **gametes**, are not produced by mitosis, but by a different kind of cell division called **meiosis**. In meiosis, the chromosomes replicate once but then divide twice, which reduces the chromosome number of each daughter cell to half that of the original cell. Also, since meiosis consists of two successive divisions, it results in the production of four daughter cells.

Although all body cells originate from one cell, the body cells in the adult organism do not all look alike or have the same function. This is because cells have the ability to develop different characteristics in a process called differentiation. Differentiation is accomplished in individual cells by the expression (activity) of some genes, and the simultaneous repression (inactivating) of others. In other words, all the information stored in DNA is not used in every cell. Instead, DNA information required for universal cell processes is active in multiple cell types, whereas information specific to one cell type is only activated in that particular kind of cell. Unraveling the mysteries of differentiation, such as the signals that activate or repress genes, is presently a hot topic of research by developmental biologists.

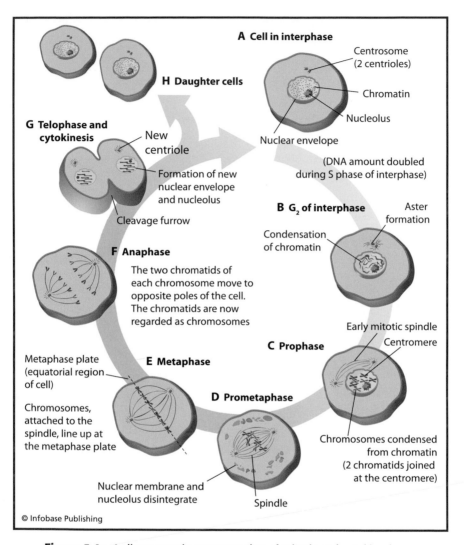

A Cell in interphase

Centrosome
(2 centrioles)

H Daughter cells

Chromatin

Nucleolus

Nuclear envelope

**G Telophase and
cytokinesis**

New
centriole

Formation of new
nuclear envelope
and nucleolus

Cleavage furrow

(DNA amount doubled
during S phase of interphase)

B G₂ of interphase

Aster
formation

Condensation
of chromatin

F Anaphase

The two chromatids of
each chromosome move to
opposite poles of the cell.
The chromatids are now
regarded as chromosomes

Early mitotic spindle

Centromere

C Prophase

Metaphase plate
(equatorial region
of cell)

E Metaphase

Chromosomes,
attached to the
spindle, line up at
the metaphase plate

D Prometaphase

Chromosomes condensed
from chromatin
(2 chromatids joined
at the centromere)

Nuclear membrane and
nucleolus disintegrate

Spindle

© Infobase Publishing

Figure 5.4   A diagrammatic representation of mitosis and cytokinesis.
(a) Interphase is a period of cell growth and when a cell carries out
its normal functions. (b) The second gap phase (G₂) is a relatively
brief interval between DNA replication and cell division, in which a
cell completes replication of its centrioles and synthesizes enzymes
that control cell division. (c) Chromatin condenses into chromosomes,
spindle fibers elongate, and nucleoli and the nuclear envelope disappear
during prophase. (d) Some of the spindle fibers attach to chromosomes,
causing them to move during prometaphase (also called late prophase).

CANCER

Cancer refers to a **malignant** tissue mass that arises from mutations in genes that regulate cell growth and division. In other words, cancer cells do not respond to normal cell cycle controls, causing them to replicate indefinitely. Cancer is the second leading cause of death in this country, and almost half of all Americans will develop cancer at some point (cardiovascular disease is the number one killer of Americans). The most common forms of cancer originate in the skin, lung, colon, stomach, prostate, breast, and urinary bladder.

Because cancer cells replicate indefinitely, they are considered "immortal." This property results, in part, from the production of telomerase, an enzyme that protects telomeres from degrading with each cell division (telomerase is not found in healthy cells). In addition, cancer cells do not display **apoptosis** (programmed cell death), a mechanism that normally eliminates damaged and unhealthy cells. Further, the altered glycocalyx of cancer cells often prevents them from being recognized and destroyed by cells of the immune system. Scientists also have shown that cancer cells do not display *density-dependent inhibition*. That is, normal animal cells growing in culture form a single layer and then usually stop dividing when they touch one another. In contrast, cancer cells keep on dividing even when crowded.

(e) Metaphase is characterized by chromosomes lining up along the midline of a cell. (f) During anaphase the spindle fibers pull sister chromatids to opposite poles of a cell. (g) Telophase can be thought of as prophase in reverse; the chromatin decondenses, new nuclear envelopes and nucleoli appear, and spindles vanish. Telophase is the end of nuclear division, but overlaps with cytokinesis, or division of the cytoplasm (note the formation of the cleavage furrow, which pinches the cell in two). (h) Completion of this cycle results in two daughter cells with identical sets of genes.

A tumor is an abnormal cell mass that develops when controls for the cell cycle malfunction. **Benign** tumors tend to grow slowly, although in an unprogrammed way. Because they express cell surface recognition proteins, their cells stick together and therefore rarely *metastasize*. Benign tumors also are surrounded by a capsule, which normally is not penetrated by blood vessels. This, in turn, keeps them from becoming much larger than a few centimeters in diameter. Benign tumors are seldom fatal, with the exception of some brain tumors. Skin moles and warts are both examples of benign tumors.

In contrast, malignant tumors grow and divide more rapidly. In addition, their cells generally lose their specialized structures and appear *undifferentiated*. For example, cells of malignant tumors often do not construct a normal cytoskeleton. As a

STEM CELLS

Stem cells are undifferentiated cells. This property makes them *pluripotent*, meaning that they have the potential to differentiate into virtually any cell type found in the body. In fact, the name "stem cell" refers to the notion that all the various cells of the body originate, or stem, from them. As a general rule, once a cell differentiates, it loses the ability to become another cell type.

Some adult tissues, such as the **dermis** of the skin, bone marrow, and brain, contain stem cells. However, because adult stem cells are already somewhat specialized, they may not have the same developmental possibilities as embryonic ones do. Nonetheless, stem cells from adult skin have been successfully induced to form nerve cells.

Embryonic stem cells have several properties that make them ideal for use in the treatment of spinal cord injuries or in various diseases, including Parkinson's disease (degeneration of certain brain cells), Alzheimer's disease (a degenerative brain disorder), diabetes mellitus (a disease of the pancreas affecting blood sugar regulation), and leukemia (a blood cell cancer). In addition to being result, they become disorganized masses that do not perform normal functions, yet still consume oxygen and produce waste products. Because these cell masses lack capsules, they often are infiltrated with blood vessels, and therefore may become quite large. As a result, malignant tumors can crush vital organs, impede blood flow, and outcompete normal tissues for nutrients. Further, the plasma membranes of malignant tumors do not function properly. For instance, they often do not express *cell adhesion molecules*, allowing cells to break free and enter the bloodstream or lymph vessels. This, in turn, allows cancer cells to invade other parts of the body and start growing new tumors, a process called **metastasis** (Figure 5.5).

Agents that cause cancer are called **carcinogens** or **mutagens**. Examples include radiation (X-rays and ultraviolet

completely undifferentiated, they grow well in culture. They also tend to induce a less vigorous immune response than adult cells, making tissue rejection less likely.

An ideal source of human stem cells would be from a very young embryo, typically in the first few days after fertilization. The reason for this is that all the cells at this stage are still undifferentiated and alike. Currently, the only source of embryonic cells is from embryos created in excess of need by fertility clinics for in vitro fertilization. However, these are rare and only available to a handful of researchers. Alternatively, the tissue that develops earliest in a human fetus suffices for treatment of some diseases, and nonliving fetuses are more common than several-day-old embryos as a consequence of legal abortions. Presently, over 100 patients afflicted with Parkinson's disease have received fetal nerve cell transplants.

The use of embryonic cells and fetal tissues is controversial. Patient advocacy groups recognize potential benefits for treating debilitating illnesses, but on the other hand, some groups object to harvesting or using human stem cells under any circumstances because the embryo is destroyed in the process. What do you think?

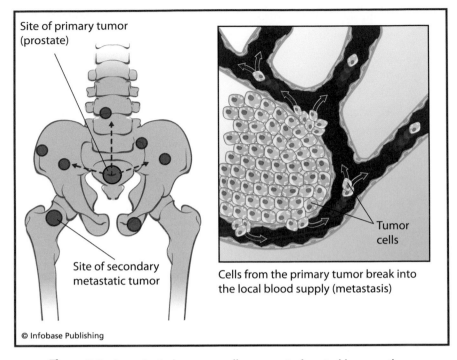

Site of primary tumor
(prostate)

Site of secondary
metastatic tumor

Tumor
cells

Cells from the primary tumor break into
the local blood supply (metastasis)

© Infobase Publishing

Figure 5.5   In metastasis, cancer cells grow out of control because the
normal checks and balances of the cell cycle, which regulate growth and
reproduction, are altered. These cells can remain in their original location
and form a tumor (a collection of cells) or metastasize, traveling through
the body, spreading the disease.

rays), physical trauma, certain viral infections, and many
chemicals (including tobacco tars). All these factors have
the capability to change DNA, which alters the expression of
genes. In some cases, carcinogens convert proto-oncogenes
to **oncogenes**. Although proto-oncogenes code for proteins
necessary for normal cell division, oncogenes allow cells to
become cancerous.

Some normal gene products aid in DNA repair, especially when subtle mistakes occur in DNA replication during
interphase. As a result, these genes act as tumor-suppressor
agents, and they can even cause cell division to stop if DNA
is damaged beyond repair by initiating apoptosis. The most

studied **tumor-suppressor gene** is the *p53* gene. Unfortunately, tumor-suppressor genes can be damaged or altered by carcinogenic agents, which can lead to the development of malignant tumors. For example, a malfunctioning *p53* gene is linked with some breast cancers. Colon cancer involves both activation of an oncogene, which leads to the formation of a polyp or benign tumor, followed by inactivation of one or more tumor-suppressor genes, which allows a malignancy to develop.

Whenever possible, surgical removal is recommended for a tumor. However, if surgery is not feasible or metastasis has occurred, radiation or chemotherapy (drugs) is usually prescribed. Both procedures target rapidly dividing cells with the aim of causing more damage to continuously dividing cancer cells than to healthy cells. However, body tissues that normally have relatively high rates of cell division, such as the lining of the gastrointestinal tract and **hair follicles**, also are negatively affected. This explains why nausea, vomiting, and hair loss are common side affects with radiation and chemotherapy.

MUTATIONS

A mutation refers to a change in the structure of DNA. This, in turn, can cause production of an abnormal protein because of the insertion of incorrect amino acids or deletion of amino acids during protein synthesis. The abnormal protein may not function properly. A consequence of a mutation can be a specific disease. For example, since enzymes and many structural components of the body are composed of proteins, mutations can lead to a variety of enzyme deficiency diseases or disorders affecting membrane transport or regulation of metabolism. Sickle-cell anemia is an example of an inherited mutation caused by the substitution of one incorrect amino acid in the entire hemoglobin molecule. Mutations can also cause cancer. Excessive exposure to ultraviolet light, X-rays, and some chemicals, such as tars in cigarette smoke, alcohol, and certain environmental pollutants, can cause mutations.

DID YOU KNOW?

Necrosis is a term that refers to the death of a cell, group of cells, or region of tissue due to an injury or disease. For instance, necrosis may result from insufficient blood supply because of a hemorrhage (broken blood vessel) or an abnormally large blood clot that blocks flow through a vessel. Consequently, affected areas do not receive adequate oxygen and nutrients, and they cannot eliminate waste products. Necrosis may also result from severe trauma or exposure to toxic chemicals and radiation (e.g., infrared, ultraviolet, and X-ray).

In contrast to uncontrolled cell death of necrosis, sometimes it is necessary for a cell to commit suicide. Apoptosis (programmed cell death) eliminates cells that are damaged beyond repair or cells that are not needed, excessive in number, or aged. During apoptosis, a series of intracellular enzymes activate in response to damaged molecules within a cell or to an appropriate external signal. The enzymes cut chromatin into many pieces and also destroy the cytoskeleton. As a result, the nuclear envelope breaks down and the plasma membrane pinches in, causing the cell and its organelles to collapse upon themselves. In this way, the damaged cellular contents do not leak out, but instead the cell shrinks and rounds up, making it more easily consumed by a phagocytic white blood cell.

CONNECTIONS

The nucleus is the largest cytoplasmic organelle and is surrounded by a double-layered envelope, consisting of inner and outer lipid bilayer membranes. It is considered the "command center" of a cell because its DNA contains the genetic code that has the instructions to produce virtually every protein in the body. Each nucleus contains one or more nucleoli, which are small, nonmembranous, dense bodies where ribosomal subunits are assembled. Chromatin consists of loosely coiled fibers of protein and DNA and contains information for protein synthesis in regions called genes.

The cell cycle refers to the series of changes that a cell undergoes from the time it forms until it reproduces. The cell cycle includes interphase, mitosis, cytoplasmic division, and differentiation. Mitosis is divided into five phases: prophase, prometaphase (also known as late prophase), metaphase, anaphase, and telophase. Meiosis is a form of nuclear division that occurs in the gonads, which reduces the chromosome number of each daughter cell by half during the formation of gametes.

A tumor is an abnormal cell mass that develops when controls for the cell cycle malfunction. Benign tumors tend to grow slowly, although in an unprogrammed way, and are generally not fatal. In contrast, malignant tumors grow and divide more rapidly, and their cells appear undifferentiated and are capable of metastasis.

6

Tissues: When Cells Get Together

THERE ARE FOUR MAJOR TYPES OF TISSUES IN THE HUMAN BODY: *epithelial*, *connective*, *muscle*, and *nervous*, which are described in Table 6.1. Tissues have diverse functions in the body, including protection, support, transport, movement, storage, and control. Because organs are made of several tissue types, an understanding of tissue structure and function will provide an appropriate foundation for a more thorough understanding of organs and organ systems and, therefore, the human body.

EPITHELIAL TISSUE

Epithelial tissues cover body surfaces, line most internal cavities and organs, and are the major components of glands. As a boundary between different environments, epithelial tissues have several different functions, including protection, absorption, secretion, filtration, excretion, and sensory reception. For example, the epithelium of the skin protects underlying tissues from mechanical and chemical damage and from bacterial invasion. In contrast, epithelial tissue lining the small intestine is specialized for absorption of nutrients, while the epithelium of glands secretes products such as saliva or digestive enzymes. Some epithelial tissues in the kidneys are specialized for the filtration of blood, and others selectively absorb substances from and secrete substances into the filtrate in order to produce urine.

Epithelial tissues have several unique characteristics. As a general rule, they are *avascular*, meaning they lack blood vessels. They therefore obtain necessary substances by diffusion from blood vessels located in underlying **connective tissues**. Epithelial cells have the capacity to reproduce readily.

TABLE 6.1

TYPE OF TISSUE	LOCATION	FUNCTION	SPECIAL CHARACTERISTICS
Epithelial	Covers body surfaces, lines internal cavities, and composes glands.	Protection, absorption, secretion, filtration, excretion, and sensory reception.	Avascular, reproduces readily, and cells are tightly packed and polarized.
Connective	Widely distributed throughout body.	Binds, supports, protects, fills spaces, stores fat, produces blood cells, and fights infection.	Widely spaced cells, extracellular matrix, and varying degrees of vascularization.
Muscle	Attaches to bones, walls of hollow organs, and the heart.	Allows body movement, propels contents of organs, and pumps blood.	Highly cellular, well vascularized, and contractile.
Nervous	Brain, spinal cord, and peripheral nerves.	Coordinates, regulates, and integrates body functions. Sensory reception and perception.	Neurons conduct electrical impulses, and neuroglia insulate and nourish neurons.

For instance, the inner lining of the small intestine is replaced about every five days. In addition, injuries to an epithelium heal quickly as new cells replace lost or damaged ones. This explains in part how an abrasion or cut in the skin heals. Epithelial cells are also tightly packed, with little intercellular space and material between them. In fact, adjacent cells are usually bound together at many points by special contacts found in the plasma membranes. This tight packing of cells makes epithelia into effective barriers.

Finally, because epithelia cover surfaces, they always have one free side; that is, a side exposed to the outside of the body or an internal cavity. This exposed side is called the **apical surface**. The opposite side, or **basal surface**, is anchored to underlying tissues by a nonliving substance called the **basement membrane**. Interestingly, the two cell surfaces (apical and basal) have different properties, resulting from different peripheral and integral proteins in their membranes. As a result, cells with distinct basal and apical surfaces are said to be "polarized," and it is this property that allows epithelial cells to transport substances unidirectionally (both absorbing and secreting). It is also common for the apical surface of epithelial cells to possess microvilli, fingerlike extensions of the plasma membrane that greatly increase surface area.

The basement membrane located underneath the basal surface is actually composed of two distinct layers. Its outer layer, the **basal lamina**, is secreted by epithelial cells, whereas the inner **reticular lamina** is made by cells of the underlying connective tissue. Together, these two layers provide support and attachment for epithelial tissues (Figure 6.1).

Types of Epithelial Tissue

Epithelial tissues are classified according to the shape of their cells. **Squamous epithelium** has flat, scalelike cells, whereas **cuboidal epithelium** has cube-shaped cells. **Columnar epithelium** has cells that are relatively tall and shaped like a column. Transitional cells change shape as the particular

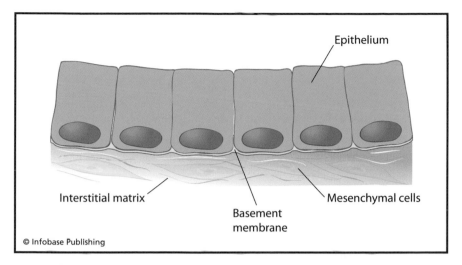

Figure 6.1 Diagrammatic view of the basement membrane. This membrane is an extracellular layer that defines an epithelial boundary and also helps reinforce epithelial sheets, resisting stretching and tearing. The basement membrane is actually two layers. The outer layer, the basal lamina, is secreted by epithelial cells, whereas the inner reticular lamina is formed by underlying connective tissue. Mesenchymal cells are found in an embryo and are the source of all connective tissues.

tissue they are located in stretches. Epithelia are also classified according to the number of cell layers they contain. For instance, **simple epithelia** are composed of a single layer of cells, whereas **stratified epithelia** are made up of multiple layers. However, sometimes a single layer of cells can appear multilayered because some of the cells do not extend all the way to the apical surface. This arrangement describes **pseudostratified epithelia**. (Figure 6.2).

Simple squamous epithelium consists of a single layer of flattened, scalelike cells, which allows substances to pass through them easily. That is why this tissue type is a common site for diffusion and filtration. For instance, simple squamous epithelia line the air sacs of the lungs and also the inside walls of blood capillaries. Simple cuboidal epithelia cover structures in the ovaries and line tubules within the kidneys and many

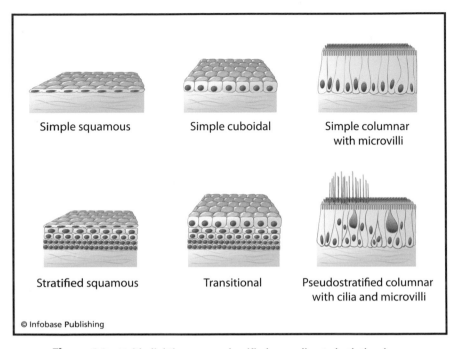

Simple squamous   Simple cuboidal   Simple columnar with microvilli

Stratified squamous   Transitional   Pseudostratified columnar with cilia and microvilli

© Infobase Publishing

Figure 6.2 Epithelial tissues are classified according to both the shape and arrangement of their cells. Squamous cells are flat while columnar cells are shaped like a column or cylinder. Tissues can consist of a single layer of cells (simple), or several layers (stratified). Pseudostratified epithelium has a single layer of cells, but appears stratified because some of the cells do not extend all the way through the tissue.

glands including the salivary glands, thyroid gland, and pancreas. Simple columnar epithelia are found in the uterus and most organs of the digestive tract, including the stomach and small intestine.

Pseudostratified columnar epithelia, which are often ciliated, line the respiratory passages and reproductive system. In the respiratory system, the cilia move mucus and trapped particles, such as dust and microorganisms, away from the lungs.

Stratified squamous epithelium contains several layers of cells, with those in the outermost layers being squamous. However, cells in the deeper layers may be more cuboidal or columnar in shape. This type of tissue lines surfaces of the mouth, throat, vagina, and anal canal. It also forms the outer layer of the skin, known as the **epidermis**.

Transitional epithelium consists of several layers of cells, which vary in appearance from cuboidal to squamous depending on the degree to which the tissue is stretched. This tissue type is found in the urinary bladder and parts of the uterus and urethra.

Epithelia also form secretory parts of glands, structures that are specialized to produce and release specific substances. Glands that secrete their products into ducts that open onto external surfaces or into internal body cavities are called exocrine glands. Examples of exocrine glands include salivary glands, **sweat glands**, pancreatic glands, **mammary glands**, and **sebaceous glands**. In contrast, glands that secrete their products (*hormones*) into tissue fluids or the bloodstream are called **endocrine glands**. These include the thyroid gland, adrenal glands, and pituitary gland.

CONNECTIVE TISSUE

Connective tissues are the most widely distributed and abundant of the four tissue types. They also have numerous and varied functions, which include binding structures, providing support and protection, serving as a framework, filling spaces, storing fat, producing blood cells, protecting against infection, and helping repair tissue damage. Connective tissues also vary widely in their degree of vascularization. **Cartilage**, for example, is essentially avascular, and ligaments and tendons are poorly vascularized. In contrast, bone is vascularized, and **adipose tissue** has a rich supply of blood vessels.

Although connective tissues display great diversity in structure and function, they all share some common properties: They are derived from an embryonic tissue called *mesenchyme*, and they are all surrounded by a nonliving extracellular matrix secreted by the connective tissue cells. Thus, unlike the other three primary tissue types that are composed mostly of cells, connective tissues are largely composed of nonliving matrix, which may widely separate living cells. However, it is this matrix that provides most connective tissues with the ability to withstand great tension and physical trauma.

The extracellular matrix is composed of protein fibers and **ground substance**. The fibers provide physical support. The strongest and most common type of fiber is composed of **collagen**. Collagen fibers are found in structures that resist pulling forces, such as tendons, which connect muscles to bones. **Elastic fibers** are composed of the protein elastin. They have a greater ability to stretch than collagen fibers and also have a great tolerance for repeated bending. **Elastic cartilage** is found in the external ear, vocal cords, and epiglottis (the flap that prevents food from entering the respiratory passages). In contrast, ground substance serves as connective tissue "glue," filling the space between cells and containing protein fibers. Depending on the type of connective tissue, ground substance can be liquid (blood), semisolid or gel-like (cartilage), or very hard (bone).

Types of Connective Tissue

Connective tissues include bone, cartilage, dense connective tissues, loose connective tissues, adipose tissue, and blood.

Bone

Bone is the most rigid connective tissue. Its living cells, called **osteocytes**, reside in cavities called **lacunae** (Figure 6.3). The lacunae are surrounded by an extracellular matrix deposited in layers arranged in concentric circles known as *lamellae*, which together form the basic structural unit of bone called an **osteon**. Many osteons glued together form a large part of the substance of bone. The hardness of bone is due to mineral salts deposited in the extracellular matrix. The matrix also contains a significant amount of collagen, which keeps the bone from becoming brittle. (Without collagen, bone would have a consistency similar to chalk. On the other hand, with only collagen, it would be more like a garden hose). Bone

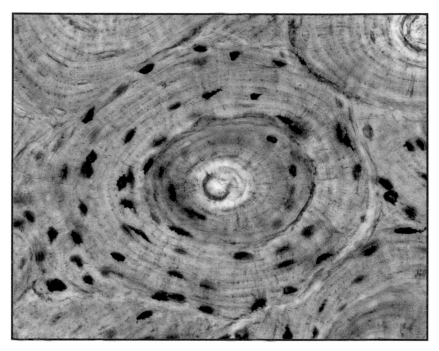

Figure 6.3 Cross section of bone showing lacunae, lamellae, and osteons.

supports body structures, protects vital organs such as the brain and heart, provides attachment sites for muscles, and stores minerals such as calcium and phosphate. Bone marrow produces blood cells.

Cartilage

Cartilage is a flexible tissue. It is made up of cells called **chondrocytes** that sit within lacunae within a matrix. There are three types of cartilage. The most abundant is **hyaline cartilage**, which provides support and flexibility. For instance, it attaches ribs to the breastbone (*sternum*), forms the voice box (*larynx*), and covers the ends of bones where they form joints. It is also found in the soft part of the nose. Elastic cartilage is more flexible than hyaline cartilage and is found in the external ear. **Fibrocartilage** forms cushionlike disks between the vertebrae of the backbone and also between bones in the knee joint.

Dense Connective Tissue

Dense connective tissue contains many tightly woven collagen fibers, which are produced by **fibroblasts**. It is found in structures that act as straps or connections, such as *tendons* (which connect muscle to bone) and *ligaments* (which connect bone to bone). It also makes up the dermis, the lower layer of skin. The fibroblasts that compose dense (and loose) connective tissue also help repair tears in body tissues. For example, when skin is cut, fibroblasts move to the area of the wound and produce collagen fibers that help close the wound and provide a surface upon which the outer layer of skin can grow.

Loose Connective Tissue

Loose connective tissues have more cells and fewer fibers than any other type of connective tissue, except for blood. The most widely distributed loose connective tissue is **areolar tissue**. It forms delicate, thin membranes throughout the body and acts as a packing material and glue. For example, it binds skin to underlying organs and also fills spaces between muscles. In addition, it wraps small blood vessels and nerves. Because of the loose and fluid nature of its extracellular matrix, it provides a reservoir of water and salts for surrounding tissues. In fact, virtually all body cells obtain nutrients from the matrix of areolar tissue, and they also release waste products into it. When a body region becomes inflamed, such as from an infection, areolar tissue takes up excess fluid like a sponge. This causes the area to swell, a condition called *edema*.

Adipose Tissue

Adipose tissue is a type of loose connective tissue that stores fat in droplets within the cytoplasm of its cells. It is found in the tissue layer beneath skin, the *subcutaneous* layer, where it insulates the body from temperature changes. Adipose tissue also cushions and protects some organs such as the kidneys, heart, and eyeballs. In addition, adipose stores fat in the abdominal membranes and hips as an energy reserve.

Blood

Blood is a special connective tissue consisting of a liquid matrix called **plasma** and several different kinds of cells. In blood, the fibers of the extracellular matrix are soluble proteins in the plasma that become visible during blood clotting. The main function of blood is to transport substances within the body, including nutrients from digested food, waste products, respiratory gases, hormones, and antibodies. Red blood cells, or **erythrocytes**, transport oxygen from the lungs to the body cells. They also carry some carbon dioxide from the cells to the lungs. White blood cells, or **leukocytes**, are responsible for fighting infections, and **platelets** are involved in blood clotting.

DID YOU KNOW?

Cartilage is avascular (lacks blood vessels), and tendons and ligaments are poorly vascularized. In addition, older chondrocytes lose their ability to divide. This explains why these three types of connective tissues heal very slowly when injured. In addition, later in life, cartilage tends to calcify so that its matrix resembles that of bone. When this happens, the tissue loses its ability to heal to any great extent.

Adipose tissue can cushion certain organs, helping hold them in place. This function becomes readily apparent in individuals who are severely malnourished and emaciated, as can happen with the eating disorder *anorexia nervosa*. If there is insufficient dietary intake of calories, the fatty encasement around the kidneys can diminish, which may cause the organs to drop lower in the body. This, in turn, can kink the ureters, blocking urine flow to the bladder. As a result, urine backs up into the kidneys, causing severe damage and ultimately renal failure.

Blood also plays an important role in temperature regulation. This is accomplished in part by altering the patterns of blood flow to different parts of the body in response to temperature changes. This is accomplished by changes in the diameter of blood vessels. In **vasodilation**, the diameter of blood vessels increases, which increases blood flow. For example, vasodilation of vessels under the skin occurs when it is necessary to release excess body heat to the external environment. This explains why skin looks flushed when someone is overheated. In contrast, **vasoconstriction** is the narrowing of blood vessels. Vasoconstriction of blood vessels under the skin conserves body heat by restricting blood flow to deep body areas, virtually bypassing skin. Because the skin is separated from deeper organs by an insulating layer of adipose tissue, heat loss through the outer layer is reduced in this case. Restricting blood flow to the skin for short periods of time does not pose a problem. However, restriction of blood flow for extended periods of time in extreme cold can lead to frostbite. This is because the temperature of the outer body layer approaches that of the external environment, which can cause skin to freeze. In addition, skin cells die if they are deprived of oxygen and nutrients for too long.

MUSCLE TISSUE

Muscle tissues are highly cellular, well vascularized, and have the ability to generate force by contracting. There are three different types of muscle tissue: *skeletal, smooth,* and *cardiac* (Figure 6.4).

Skeletal muscle is attached to bones and is under voluntary control. Under a microscope, its cells are cylindrical in shape and reveal alternating light and dark patterns called *striations*.

Figure 6.4   *(opposite page)* Muscle is a type of contractile tissue. (a) Skeletal muscle is striated and the cells have multiple nuclei. (b) Smooth muscle is not striated. (c) Cardiac muscle, which is also striated, has structures called intercalated disks joining adjacent cells.

Because of the striations, skeletal muscle is also called *striated muscle*. Skeletal muscle is responsible for generating movements of the limbs, trunk, and head, as well as allowing us to make facial expressions, talk, chew, swallow, breathe, and write. In addition, skeletal muscle helps maintain posture, stabilizes joints, and generates heat (shivering is the result of involuntary contractions of skeletal muscle).

Smooth muscle cells lack striations, and this type of muscle is generally not under voluntary control. However, disciplined individuals who practice yoga or biofeedback can develop the ability to control some smooth muscle actions. Smooth muscle is found in the walls of blood vessels (except capillaries) and the airways (bronchioles), where its contraction reduces flow of blood or air, respectively. Smooth muscle is also located in the walls of hollow organs, such as the stomach, intestines, uterus, and urinary bladder, where its contractions aid in propelling the contents of the organs.

Cardiac muscle is only found in the walls of the heart, and its contractions are responsible for pumping the blood through the body. Like skeletal muscle, its cells have a striated appearance when observed with a microscope. However, like smooth muscle, its contractions are generally considered involuntary. A unique anatomical property of cardiac muscle is a specialized junction that electrically connects heart cells, thereby allowing a rapid conduction of electrical impulses throughout the heart muscle. This type of cell junction is called an *intercalated disk*.

NERVOUS TISSUE

Nervous tissue makes up the brain, spinal cord, and peripheral nerves, which coordinate, regulate, and integrate many body functions. Nervous tissue consists of two major cell types: neurons and neuroglia. **Neurons** are the cells that generate and conduct electrical impulses, sometimes over substantial distances. These impulses influence other neurons, muscles, and glands. Some neurons have the ability to convert external

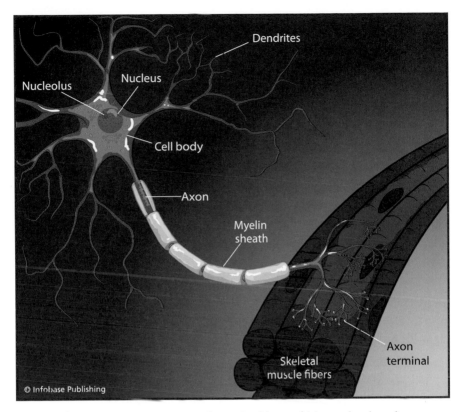

Figure 6.5 Most neurons have dendrites, which receive impulses from adjacent neurons, a cell body, which contains the cell nucleus and organelles, and an axon, which transmits impulses from the cell body to adjacent neurons or to a muscle. The axon may be covered by a myelin sheath, which insulates it and increases the impulse transmission speed.

stimuli, such as light, heat, or sound, into electrical signals that are recognized by the brain. Most neurons have a cell body, dendrites, and an axon. The *cell body* contains a nucleus and most organelles. *Dendrites* are highly branched processes of the cell body that receive impulses from adjacent neurons and carry them toward the cell body. The *axon* of a neuron is a single long process that carries impulses away from the cell body toward adjacent neurons or muscles (Figure 6.5).

Neuroglia do not generate and conduct nerve impulses as do neurons. However, they are essential for normal neuronal function. Some neuroglia wrap themselves repeatedly around an axon, forming layers of membrane called a **myelin sheath**. This sheath acts as electrical insulation, which increases the rate at which impulses are conducted (over 109 yards, or 100 m per second for some neurons). Other neuroglial cells are phagocytic, and still others provide neurons with nutrients by connecting them to blood vessels.

YOUR HEALTH: MULTIPLE SCLEROSIS

The importance of neuroglia to nerve transmission becomes evident when studying the disease multiple sclerosis (MS), a chronic, progressive, degenerative disorder that affects nerve fibers in the central nervous system. This disease is the most common neurological cause of debilitation in young people, with an average age of onset between 18 and 35 years. It affects 500,000 people in the United States and is more common in women and in Caucasians. MS is classified as an *autoimmune disease*, which means the immune system inappropriately attacks "self cells." This immune response is apparently triggered by genetic, environmental, and/or viral factors.

In MS, the neuroglial cells that wrap around axons in the central nervous system are attacked. This, in turn, leads to progressive destruction of the myelin sheaths. As a result, there is substantial short-circuiting of electrical signals, and eventually impulse conduction ceases. Symptoms vary depending on the specific nerve fibers that are affected, but they typically include reduced vision, muscle weakness, clumsiness, and urinary incontinence. Interestingly, neuronal axons are not damaged and may even show some recovery by increasing their number of ion channels. This apparently accounts for periods of *remission* (temporary recovery). However, these are typically followed by further cycles of relapse as additional myelin is destroyed. Eventually, blindness and paralysis may occur.

CONNECTIONS

Groups of cells that are similar in structure and function are called tissues. The four major tissue types in the human body are epithelial, connective, muscle, and nervous. Tissues have diverse functions, which include protection, support, transport, movement, storage, and control.

Epithelial tissues cover body surfaces, line most internal cavities and organs, and are the major component of glands. As a boundary between different environments, epithelial tissues have several different functions, including protection, absorption, secretion, filtration, excretion, and sensory reception. Connective tissues, the most abundant tissue type, bind structures, provide support and protection, serve as a framework, fill spaces, store fat, produce blood cells, protect against infection, and help repair tissue damage. Connective tissues include bone, cartilage, dense connective tissue (tendons and ligaments), loose connective tissue (areolar and adipose), and blood. Muscle tissues are highly cellular, well vascularized, and have the ability to generate force by contracting. The three different types of muscle tissue are skeletal, smooth, and cardiac. Nervous tissue makes up the brain, spinal cord, and peripheral nerves, which coordinate, regulate, and integrate many body functions. Nervous tissue consists of two major cell types: neurons (the cells that generate and conduct electrical impulses) and supporting neuroglia.

7

Skin: An Exemplary Organ

TWO OR MORE TISSUE TYPES MAY BE ORGANIZED INTO MORE complex structures called organs, which perform specific functions for the body. Many organs, such as skin, are composed of all four tissue types: epithelial, connective, muscle, and nerve. Although skin is sometimes referred to as the **cutaneous membrane**, it is by definition an organ. In fact, skin is one of the largest organs of the body. In an average adult, it weighs 9 to 11 pounds (4 to 5 kilograms, or kg), accounting for about 7% of total body weight. Along with its derivatives (sweat glands, sebaceous glands, hair, and nails) and accessory structures (blood vessels and nerves), skin is part of the integumentary system. (The word *integument* refers to a covering.)

FUNCTIONS OF SKIN

Skin is absolutely essential for **homeostasis**, the ability of the body to maintain a relatively constant internal environment. A primary function of skin is forming a barrier that protects the body from dehydration. In fact, the biggest threat to survival for terrestrial animals is dehydration, and the waterproof nature of skin keeps fluids and other important substances inside. Skin also protects the entire body from physical or external injury (bumps, abrasions, and cuts), as well as chemical damage (acids and bases). In addition, skin shields us from continual bacterial invasion and ultraviolet radiation in sunlight.

The skin plays an important role in temperature regulation. This is accomplished with its rich blood supply and sweat glands, which are controlled by the nervous system. Because sweat contains water, salts, and urea, one could argue that the integumentary system has an excretory function. Skin also synthesizes vitamin D from modified cholesterol molecules when exposed to ultraviolet radiation (actually vitamin D is not a true vitamin because individuals with adequate exposure to sunlight do not require dietary supplementation). Vitamin D is necessary for the small intestine to absorb dietary calcium. That is why a lack of this vitamin can lead to the disease *rickets*, a disorder characterized by inadequate mineralization of bones. Symptoms include bowed legs and deformities of the pelvis, skull, and rib cage. Finally, skin contains components of the nervous system that detect temperature, touch, pressure, and pain stimuli. As a result, skin provides us with a great deal of information about our external environment.

STRUCTURE OF SKIN

Skin has two tissue layers: the epidermis and dermis (Figure 7.1). The outer layer, the epidermis, is composed of stratified squamous epithelium. Beneath the epidermis is the thicker dermis, which is made of connective tissue. As is true for all epithelial tissues, blood vessels are absent in the epidermis but present in the dermis. Although the two skin layers are firmly connected, a burn or friction can cause them to separate, forming a *blister*.

The skin's **subcutaneous tissue**, or *hypodermis*, is technically not part of skin. However, it shares many of the skin's protective functions. The hypodermis consists mostly of adipose tissue and some areolar connective tissue. It helps anchor skin, stores fat, and acts as thermal and mechanical insulation.

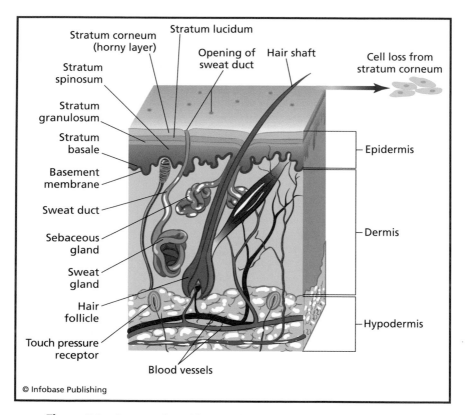

Figure 7.1 Cross section of human skin. The skin is made up of two layers, the epidermis and the dermis. The outer layer, the epidermis, is composed of stratified squamous epithelial cells. The dermis, which is below the epidermis, is composed of connective tissue.

Because of its extensive adipose tissue, the hypodermis can thicken when one gains weight, which occurs in a sex-specific manner in adults. For instance, females tend to accumulate excess fat in the thighs, hips, and breasts, whereas men first show increased adipose tissue in the abdomen.

Epidermis

The epidermis is composed of four different cell types and is organized into four or five layers, or *strata*. The most abundant cell type is the **keratinocyte**. It produces a fibrous protein called **keratin** that gives the epidermis its protective properties. Keratinocytes arise in the deepest layer of the epidermis by mitosis and are gradually pushed outward toward the skin surface. During this migration, the cells flatten, fill with keratin, and die. In other words, the outer layer of skin is actually composed of dead cells, and millions of dead keratinocytes are rubbed off every day (it has been estimated that we lose about 40 pounds, or 18 kg, of skin cells in an average lifetime). The total life span of a keratinocyte, from its formation to being rubbed off, is 25 to 45 days. In addition, persistent friction can increase the rate of cell production and keratin formation, leading to a thickening of the epidermis called a *callus*.

Melanocytes are cells located near the base of the epidermis. They produce a dark-colored pigment called melanin, which influences skin color and also absorbs ultraviolet radiation. After melanin is released from melanocytes, it is then

HOMEOSTASIS

Arguably, homeostasis is the single most important concept of physiology, a branch of biology that deals with the functions and vital processes of living organisms or their parts. In fact, the concept of homeostasis is used as a central model to explain the complex processes of animal physiology. During the late nineteenth century, the French physiologist Claude Bernard wrote, "All the vital mechanisms, however varied they may be, have only one object, that of preserving constant the condition of life in the inner environment." In the early twentieth century, the American physiologist Walter Cannon coined the word *homeostasis* ("stable condition") to describe Bernard's concept of the inner environment. Thinking in terms of homeostasis provides a clearer understanding of how and why the human body functions the way it does. In other words, all the cells, tissues, organs, and systems work together to maintain a relatively constant internal environment.

transferred to keratinocytes, where it accumulates over the nucleus and forms a "pigment shield." A third cell type, **Langerhans cells**, are *macrophages* (white blood cells capable of phagocytosis). They originate in bone marrow and migrate to the epidermis, where they recognize and ingest foreign substances such as bacteria. In this regard, they play a role in immunity. Finally, **Merkel cells**, present at the epidermal-dermal junction, are associated with sensory nerve endings, forming *Merkel disks*, which function as sensory receptors for touch.

The deepest epidermal layer is the **stratum basale**, which is firmly attached to the dermis. It mainly consists of a single layer of cuboidal cells capable of rapid cell division. About one-fifth of the cells in this layer are melanocytes. There is also an occasional Merkel cell in this stratum. Sometimes invasion by a *papilloma virus* causes a dramatic increase in the rate of cell division in this layer. This, in turn, causes growth of a wart, which is a type of *benign tumor*.

The next layer is the **stratum spinosum** ("spiny layer"). It contains several layers of cuboidal cells, with scattered melanin granules and Langerhans cells. The **stratum granulosum** ("granular layer") consists of three to five layers of flattened cells containing *keratohyalin*, a substance that contributes to the formation of keratin. All the cells above this layer die because they are too far from dermal capillaries to obtain adequate nutrients.

The **stratum lucidum** ("clear layer") contains three to four layers of flattened dead cells. This layer is found only in the palms of the hands and soles of the feet, areas known as "thick skin." The outermost layer is the **stratum corneum** ("horny layer"). It consists of 20 to 30 layers of flat, dead cells completely filled with keratin. It is this layer that prevents water loss and protects from us from biological, chemical, and physical insults. Dandruff occurs when dry patches of epidermal cells flake off the scalp. This affliction is most common in middle age and is also associated with stress and a high-fat diet.

Dermis

The dermis lies below the epidermis, and it corresponds to animal hides used to make leather products. Unlike the epidermal layer, the dermis does not wear away. This explains why tattoos—ink droplets injected into the dermal layer—are relatively permanent. The dermis also differs from the epidermis in that it contains nerves, sensory receptors, blood vessels, hair follicles, sebaceous glands, and sweat glands.

The dermis is made up of the **papillary layer** and the **reticular layer**. The thinner outer papillary layer consists of loose (areolar) connective tissue with collagen and elastic fibers. Its outer surface forms obvious folds called *dermal papillae*. Many of these papillae contain receptors for touch and pain. In addition, these folds reach up to the epidermis, causing ridges on the surface of skin that increase friction, thereby enhancing the gripping ability of hands and feet. The specific patterns of papillary folds are genetically determined. Because the ridges on the fingertips have a rich supply of sweat pores, they may leave unique *fingerprints*, which are essentially outlines of sweat, on the surfaces they touch.

The deeper and thicker reticular layer is composed of dense connective tissue. In the extracellular matrix, it contains a combination of collagen and elastic fibers that allow skin to stretch and then return to its original shape. However, substantial body weight gain, as with pregnancy or obesity, can tear the dermis, resulting in visible lines called *stretch marks*. Also, the resilience of skin decreases with age as collagen fibers stiffen and elastic fibers lose their elasticity. These effects, along with a reduction in the ability of the dermis to hold moisture, produce wrinkles and sagging skin, which usually first become apparent by a person's late forties. The reticular layer also contains blood vessels, sweat and sebaceous glands, and receptors for the sensation of deep pressure.

Figure 7.2   Skin color is determined by the pigment melanin. Melanin is produced by cells called melanocytes and is distrbuted to other cells in the skin. A person with more melanin will have a darker skin color than a person with less.

SKIN COLOR

Two main factors contribute to skin color: the quantity and distribution of pigments (melanin and **carotene**) in the skin and blood flow. Melanin is a skin pigment made of amino acids. Its color ranges from reddish brown to black. Although melanin is only produced by melanocytes, it is continually released by exocytosis from these cells. Surrounding cells subsequently accumulate the pigment by endocytosis. Interestingly, all people have roughly the same number of melanocytes. That means variations in skin color are due to differences in the form and amount of melanin produced and in the way it is dispersed (Figure 7.2).

The most important factor in determining melanin production is a person's genetic predisposition; that is, particular characteristics inherited from one's parents. However, melanocytes also are stimulated by exposure of the skin to sunlight, causing them to increase their production of melanin. This response helps protect DNA when there is an increased exposure to ultraviolet radiation. This process is also responsible for the development of a tan. However, excessive exposure to sunlight causes clumping of elastic fibers, which leads to wrinkles and leathery-looking skin. More importantly, excessive exposure to ultraviolet light temporarily suppresses the immune system and can also alter DNA enough to cause skin cancer (described in further detail in Chapter 9). The protective nature of melanin is illustrated by the fact that dark-skinned people seldom have skin cancer, whereas this disease is more common in light-skinned individuals. Freckles and moles are local accumulations of melanin. **Albinism** is an inherited disorder in which melanocytes are incapable of producing melanin.

Carotene is a yellow orange pigment that can influence skin color. It is found in many food items such as carrots, apricots, and oranges. It tends to accumulate in the stratum corneum and in fatty tissues of the dermis. Its color is most obvious in the palms of the hands and soles of the feet and is most intense when a large amount of carotene-rich foods have been consumed.

SCARS

Scars often form following a break in skin. They do not develop when an injury is confined to the epidermis. However, they can form when damage or a surgical incision penetrates into the dermis and scar tissue can appear. It results when collagen-producing cells increase their activity in response to tissue damage. In turn, the newly produced material is pushed to the skin surface. Consequently, scar tissue lacks an epidermal layer. Therefore, when compared to normal skin, scars usually have denser collagen fibers, fewer blood vessels, and no hair.

Hemoglobin is a red pigment found in red blood cells. The pinkish hue of fair skin is due to the reddish color of oxygenated hemoglobin in blood circulating through dermal capillaries. Because Caucasian skin contains relatively small amounts of melanin, the almost transparent epidermis allows the color of underlying hemoglobin to show through.

Specific circulation patterns of blood flow can also influence skin color. For instance, embarrassment increases blood flow to the skin, particularly in the face and neck regions. This is what leads to blushing. An increase in blood flow can also be caused by high blood pressure, inflammation, or an allergic response. In contrast, a sudden fright or anger can cause a rapid drop in blood flow to the skin, causing its color to blanch. Pale skin can also indicate low blood pressure (*hypotension*), anemia (low red blood cell count), or impaired blood flow.

In addition, hemoglobin changes its color when it releases oxygen. Consequently, poorly oxygenated blood causes skin to take on a bluish hue, a condition known as **cyanosis**. Melanin masks the appearance of cyanosis in dark-skinned people. However, it can still be detected by looking at the color of fingernail beds. Cyanosis is common during heart failure or extreme breathing disorders.

Jaundice, which turns skin and eyes yellow, occurs when bile pigments, such as bilirubin, are deposited in body tissues (Figure 7.3). Bilirubin is formed by the liver during the breakdown of worn-out or damaged red blood cells. Thus, jaundice usually indicates a problem with the liver. However, jaundice is common in newborns (called *physiological jaundice*), appearing two or three days after birth in over 50% of babies. This occurs because fetal red blood cells are short-lived and break down rapidly following birth so they can be replaced with adult red blood cells. Frequently, an infant's liver is unable to process the resulting bilirubin fast enough to prevent its accumulation in blood. Usually physiological jaundice in babies is not harmful and disappears by one to two weeks of age, and in most cases an increase in the supply of breast milk or formula is

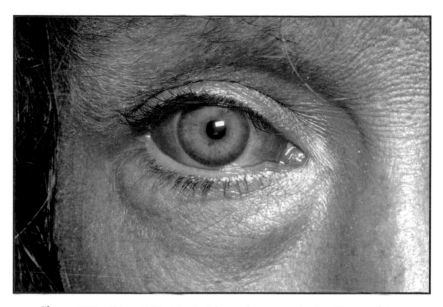

Figure 7.3 When bilirubin builds up in excess in the liver and is distributed to other cells, a condition called jaundice develops. Jaundice results in a yellowish pigment in the skin and eyes.

recommended. However, high levels of bilirubin can cause deafness or brain damage in some infants. These complications can be prevented by lowering bilirubin using phototherapy for a few days (blue light helps break down bilirubin in the skin).

CONNECTIONS

Skin is one of the largest organs of the body and, along with its derivatives (sweat glands, sebaceous glands, hair, and nails) and accessory structures (blood vessels and nerves), forms the integumentary system. The skin forms a barrier that protects the body from dehydration, as well as from physical and chemical damage. In addition, it shields us from continual bacterial invasion and ultraviolet radiation.

(continues)

(continued)

The two tissue layers of the skin are the epidermis and dermis. The epidermis is composed of stratified squamous epithelium, which contains keratinocytes, melanocytes, Langerhans cells, and Merkel cells. The tough, fibrous protein keratin accumulates in keratinocytes, providing them with their protective qualities. The dermis has two layers: the thinner outer papillary layer of loose (areolar) connective tissue and the deeper, thicker reticular layer, composed of dense connective tissue.

Two main factors contribute to skin color: the quantity and distribution of pigments in the skin and blood flow. The most important factor in determining melanin production is a person's genetic code. In addition, melanocytes are stimulated by exposure of skin to sunlight, causing them to increase their production of melanin. Specific circulation patterns of blood flow can also influence skin color.

8

Skin Derivatives

THE INTEGUMENTARY SYSTEM INCLUDES A NUMBER OF DIVERSE structures derived from the epidermis of skin, including hair, nails, sebaceous glands, and sweat glands. Each of these structures has a role in maintaining homeostasis.

HAIR

Hair is an outgrowth of skin that is unique to mammals. Its main function is to provide thermal insulation. In this capacity, however, the hairs sparsely scattered over the human body are essentially useless. Nonetheless, human hair does provide some important functions. For instance, it protects the scalp from ultraviolet rays and physical injury. Eyelashes shield the eyes and cause reflex blinking when unexpectedly touched, and hair lining the inside of the nares (nostrils) and ear canals keep out foreign particles. In addition, hair has a significant sensory role because receptors associated with follicles are sensitive to touch.

For humans, hair is present on all skin surfaces except the palms of the hands, soles of the feet, lips, nipples, and parts of the external genitalia. Humans have three different types of hair: lanugo, vellus, and terminal. **Lanugo** is the soft, fine hair that covers a fetus beginning around the third or fourth month after conception. It falls off about a month before birth, and is replaced by a second coat that is shed a few months later. Vellus hair is also soft and fine. However, unlike lanugo, it grows and persists throughout life, covering most of the body surface. Terminal hair is thick and strong. It forms eyebrows and eyelashes and is found on the scalp. During adolescence, in response to changing hormone levels, many vellus hairs of the armpits and pubic area are replaced with terminal hairs. In males, the same is true for the face, chest, legs, forearms, back, and shoulders.

Each terminal hair consists of a central core called the *medulla* (which fine hair lacks) (Figure 8.1). The medulla is surrounded by the *cortex*, which in turn is enclosed by a **cuticle**. The cuticle is formed by a single layer of cells that overlap one another like shingles on a roof. This arrangement helps keep hairs from matting or tangling with each other. The cuticle can wear away with continual exposure to the elements and abrasion, allowing the underlying cortex to frizz, forming "split

HAIR COLOR

Hair color, like skin color, is genetically determined by the amount and type of pigment produced. The pigment accumulates in the cortex of the hairs. For instance, where abundant melanin is present, hair is dark in color. In contrast, lighter hair color results when little melanin is synthesized. Interestingly, true red hair depends on a separate reddish pigment, which can also influence the overall effect of melanin. For instance, auburn hair is produced by a combination of red pigment mixed with relatively large amounts of melanin. In contrast, strawberry blond hair results when red pigment mixes with little melanin. Gray hair, associated with age, is actually caused by a decrease in the production of melanin and a corresponding increase in the number and size of air pockets in the hair shaft. Light striking the air pockets gives hair a gray sheen.

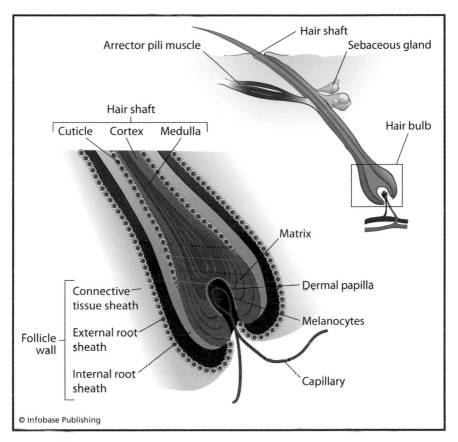

Figure 8.1   Structure of a hair and hair follicle. The region of a hair that projects from the skin is the shaft, whereas the embedded portion is the root. The hair follicle extends from the epidermis into the dermis, and its deep end is expanded, forming a hair bulb (enlarged in the diagram). Hair is produced in the bulb by active cell division in a single layer of epidermal cells called the matrix, which is nourished by a knot of capillaries in the dermal papilla. The hair shaft has a central core, the medulla (consisting of large cells and air spaces), which is surrounded by the cortex (several layers of flattened cells). The outermost cuticle is formed from a single layer of cells.

ends." The cuticle can also be damaged by exposure to chlorinated water in swimming pools.

Hair has both a *shaft* and a *root*. The shaft projects above the surface of the skin. In contrast, the root extends below the surface into the dermis, where it is embedded in a group of cells called a hair follicle. The follicle is really a compound structure, meaning it is composed of several parts. Its inner layer is a flexible sheath composed of epithelial cells that are responsible for producing hair. The outer layer is composed of dermal connective tissue. It provides blood vessels and physical reinforcement. The inferior end (bottom) of a hair follicle is enlarged, forming a structure called the hair bulb. Each **hair bulb** is wrapped by a knot of sensory nerve endings called the **hair root plexus**. This anatomical arrangement allows hair to act as a sensitive touch receptor permitting us, for instance, to feel insects crawling on our skin (hopefully before they have a chance to sting or bite us).

Hair is formed by division of cells in the matrix, a growth zone located in the hair bulb. The matrix displays active mitosis because it is continuous with the stratum basale, the epidermal layer of skin capable of cell division. The newly formed cells are nourished by blood vessels located in the **papilla**, which is an indentation of the dermal connective tissue at the base of the follicle. As daughter cells continue to divide, they are pushed farther away from the growing region and also become keratinized. Shortly thereafter, they die. Thus, the bulk of hair is composed of nonliving cells.

Hair growth depends on several factors, including nutritional status, gender, and age, as well as circulating levels of some hormones. For instance, poor nutrition results in poor hair growth. In addition, the hormone testosterone encourages growth of hair. Although scalp hair typically grows an average of 0.08 inches (2 mm) per week, each follicle goes through a series of growth cycles. Initially, there is an *active phase*, which generally lasts two to six years. This is followed by a *resting phase*, where the follicle is inactive for several months. Following the resting phase, the matrix proliferates again, forming a new hair that will replace the old one, which has already fallen out or will be pushed out. Because follicles generally spend more time in an active phase, we only shed about 90 hairs from our scalp each day. Interestingly, the active phase for eyebrow hair is only three to four months long. This explains why eyebrow hair is much shorter than scalp hair.

Hair growth is generally fastest from the teen years to the forties. After that, it slows down, and hairs are not replaced as fast as they are shed. This leads to hair thinning, which occurs in both sexes. However, true baldness, usually known as **male pattern baldness**, is a genetically determined condition influenced by the presence of male hormones. True baldness is caused by a delayed-action gene that is turned on in adulthood, thereby changing the response of hair follicles to circulating levels of testosterone. As a result, hair follicles shrink, and the length of time spent in a growth cycle decreases. In fact, growth cycles can become so short that hair does not have a chance to emerge before it is shed. In addition, thick terminal hairs are replaced by soft, fine, vellus hairs. This change occurs in a characteristic pattern, beginning at the forehead and temple, and eventually reaching the crown. Interestingly, a drug originally used to treat high blood pressure (minoxidil) was accidentally found to stimulate hair

GOOSE BUMPS

The **arrector pili muscles** are tiny, smooth muscles in the dermis attached to hair follicles. If a person is emotionally upset or cold, nerve impulses may stimulate this muscle to contract, causing it to pull on a follicle, thereby decreasing the follicle's angle with the skin surface. This, in turn, generates goose bumps. Although this action does not play a significant role in humans, it does keep other mammals warm in cold weather by increasing the thickness of their insulation. Contraction of arrector pili muscles is also used for body language signals in some animals. For instance, a scared cat looks larger when its fur stands on end, and a dog sends a clear message that it should not be touched when it raises the hair on the back of its neck while baring its teeth.

growth in some individuals. The lotion appears to work by increasing blood flow to the scalp, thereby stimulating the activity of existing follicles.

CUTANEOUS GLANDS

The cutaneous (skin) glands are *exocrine glands*. These glands secrete their products to the skin surface via ducts. The two main types of cutaneous glands are sebaceous glands and sweat glands. Both reside almost entirely in the dermis but are formed by cells of the stratum basale, an epidermal layer.

Sebaceous Glands

Sebaceous glands, or oil glands, are found all over the body except on the palms of the hands and soles of the feet. Although they are epidermal derivatives, the secretory part of the gland is located in the dermis. In some cases, the glands open directly onto the skin surface. However, in most instances, they open into hair follicles.

Sebaceous glands secrete an oily substance called **sebum**, which is made of fats, cholesterol, protein, and salts. Sebum lubricates the hair and skin. It also protects skin against desiccation, or drying out. In addition, sebum contains antibacterial chemicals that help prevent bacteria present on the skin surface from invading deeper regions. Unfortunately, the ducts of oil glands can become blocked, allowing sebum and bacteria to accumulate, which results in **acne**.

Sweat Glands

Sweat glands, or *sudoriferous glands*, are widely distributed in the skin. In fact, each person has about 2.5 million of them. There are two main types of sweat glands: *eccrine* and *apocrine*. **Eccrine glands** produce their secretions in coiled structures located in the dermis and then dump their contents (sweat) directly on the skin surface via a pore. They are most numerous in the skin of the forehead, palms, and soles. In contrast, they are absent in the lips, eardrums, nail beds, and portions of the external genitalia.

Sweat is mostly composed of water. It also contains some salts, lactic acid, vitamin C, and metabolic wastes such as urea and ammonia. The principal function of sweat is to help regulate body temperature through the evaporation of water on the skin surface. In fact, on a hot day a quart (approximately 1 L) or more of body water can easily be lost in this way. In addition, the slightly acidic pH of sweat inhibits growth of bacteria.

Apocrine glands are a type of sweat gland located mainly in the armpits and pubic region. Apocrine glands are usually larger than eccrine glands, and they empty their contents into hair follicles. Although their secretion contains all the substances present in eccrine sweat, they also contain additional fatty acids and proteins. These substances make the secretion more *viscous* (thick), and also give it a whitish yellowish color. Apocrine secretions are typically odorless, but bacterial action on the skin surface converts the proteins and fats into compounds that release an unpleasant odor. Antiperspirants are designed to inhibit such secretions, whereas deodorants mask the odor.

Apocrine glands do not function until puberty, at which time they are stimulated by an increase in levels of sex hormones (testosterone and estrogen). Although the exact function of apocrine glands is not known, they generally become most active when a person is emotionally upset or excited, such as when frightened, in pain, or sexually aroused. Apocrine glands also enlarge and shrink with the phases of a woman's menstrual cycle. It is therefore unlikely these glands play a significant role in temperature regulation. Instead, it is generally assumed that apocrine glands are analogous to the sexual scent glands of other animals, and they may also play a role during a *fight-or-flight response*. It has been suggested that pubic and axillary (underarm) hair helps disperse the odor of apocrine secretions; that is, it enhances the spread of one's scent.

Ceruminous glands are modified apocrine glands found in the lining of the external ear canal. They secrete a thick, sticky substance called **cerumen**, or earwax. Along with tiny hairs in the ear canal, this substance deters insects and blocks the entry of foreign substances.

Mammary glands are modified sweat glands specialized to secrete milk. Although they are present in both sexes, mammary glands normally function only in females. In nonpregnant women, the glandular structure is largely undeveloped, and the duct system is rudimentary. However, under stimulation of the hormone *prolactin*, which is secreted from the pituitary gland during pregnancy, the glandular tissue develops the ability to produce milk.

NAILS

Nails are protective coverings on the ends of the fingers and toes. Like hair, nails are modified skin tissue (stratified squamous epithelium) that has been hardened by the protein keratin. However, nails differ from hair in that they grow continuously. Also, compared to hair, nail growth is relatively slow. Whereas hair can grow 5 to 6 inches (12.7 to 15.2 cm) per year, fingernails grow about 1.5 inches (3.8 cm) per year, and toenails about 0.5 inches (1.3 cm) or so.

Nail cells form in a region called the *nail root*, which is embedded in skin (Figure 8.2). The growing region is the **lunula**, the whitish, crescent–shaped area at the base of a nail. As a nail develops, it slides forward over a layer of epithelium, the nail bed, which is continuous with the stratum basale. The free edge of a nail extends over the tip of a finger or toe and is the part that gets trimmed. The border of a nail is overlapped with skin folds, and the proximal nail fold is called the cuticle. Most of a nail appears pink due to the presence of blood vessels in the dermis below. The lunula, however, looks white because it has a thickened matrix that obscures underlying tissue.

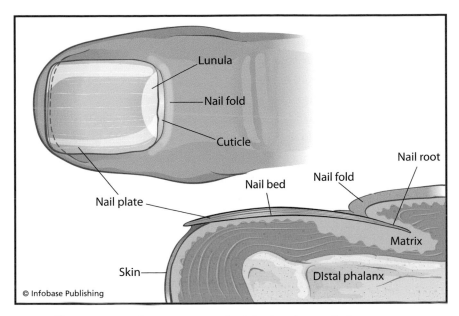

Figure 8.2 Nails are composed of hardened, stratified squamous epithelial cells. Nails form in the nail root and grow along the nail bed. The cuticle is made up of the proximal nail fold and the white, crescent-shaped area, which is called the lunula.

ORGAN SYSTEM INTEGRATION

No system in the body acts independently of the others. That is, all systems must be integrated in order to maintain homeostasis, and the integumentary system is no exception. Recall that skin is able to synthesize vitamin D when exposed to sunlight. However, this form of vitamin D does not have significant biological activity. Rather, it must be metabolized into an active form by a chemical modification in the liver, followed by a second modification in the kidneys. Vitamin D promotes absorption of dietary calcium by the small intestine. In turn, calcium is necessary for the proper formation of bones and teeth, as well as for blood clotting and the normal function of nerve and muscle tissues. Thus, by providing the body with vitamin D, the integumentary system is linked to the activity of the digestive, skeletal, muscular, nervous, cardiovascular, and renal systems.

The integumentary system also contains receptors sensitive to touch, pressure, temperature, and pain. These receptors provide the nervous system with important information about our external environment. In return the nervous system controls the activity of sweat glands and blood flow, thereby using the skin as a means to help regulate body temperature. Further, the activity of sebaceous and apocrine glands is influenced by sex hormones that are released from the endocrine system. Thus, the integumentary system is also integrated with the endocrine and reproductive systems.

CONNECTIONS

Structures derived from the epidermis of skin include hair, nails, sebaceous glands, and sweat glands. Hair is a skin outgrowth that is unique to mammals. It protects the scalp from ultraviolet rays and mechanical bumps, keeps foreign particles out of the respiratory tract, and has a sensory role.

Sebaceous glands secrete sebum, an oily substance that lubricates hair and inhibits the growth of bacteria. Eccrine glands produce sweat, which helps regulate body temperature through the evaporation of water on the skin surface. Apocrine glands are a type of sweat gland, mainly located in the armpits and pubic region. They do not function until puberty, and are assumed to be analogous to the sexual scent glands of other animals. Ceruminous glands are modified apocrine glands found in the lining of the external ear canal that produce earwax. Mammary glands are modified sweat glands specialized to secrete milk.

9

Common Skin Disorders

THERE ARE OVER 1,000 DIFFERENT AILMENTS OF THE SKIN. THE most common skin disorders result from allergies and from bacterial, viral, and fungal infections. Less common, but more serious, skin problems include burns and cancers.

ALLERGIES

An **allergy**, or *hypersensitivity*, occurs when a normally harmless substance, called an *allergen*, evokes an inappropriate immune response. It is the reaction of the immune system that causes tissue damage or other symptoms. There are two main types of allergic responses, which are distinguished by how quickly they occur and also by the specific immune response.

An **immediate hypersensitivity** describes a response (*anaphylaxis*) that occurs within seconds or minutes after contacting an allergen, such as the allergic response to bee venom, dust, pollen, or certain food items. The primary immune culprits for many immediate hypersensitivities are **mast cells** and **basophils**, white blood cells that release **histamine** and other inflammatory chemicals when specific antibodies on their surface bind to an allergen. Although these chemicals play a beneficial role during an acute inflammation caused by an infection, they are inappropriately released during an immediate hypersensitivity. Histamine causes small blood vessels in the area of exposure to dilate (widen) and become leaky. As a result, the affected region becomes red and swollen in response to increased blood flow and to fluid accumulation

YOUR HEALTH: ANAPHYLACTIC SHOCK

Often an immediate hypersensitivity is simply an annoyance, as with hay fever, which is an allergic response to ragweed. However, in some instances, an allergy may be life threatening, such as with a bee sting or drug injection, because an allergen directly enters the bloodstream. In sensitive individuals, exposure to certain foods, such as peanuts, can also produce a potentially deadly reaction. In these cases, reaction to the allergen may lead to a *systemic*, or body-wide, response called *anaphylactic shock*. In anaphylactic shock, mast cells and basophils throughout the body are inappropriately stimulated to release histamine and other chemicals. As a result, there is a sudden dilation of blood vessels accompanied by a loss of fluid from the bloodstream, which leads to circulatory collapse. In addition, airways called bronchioles constrict, making it difficult to breathe. This condition may be fatal if untreated. Individuals suffering from anaphylactic shock are usually given an injection of epinephrine (also called adrenaline), a hormone that quickly reverses the histamine-mediated events by constricting blood vessels (which raises blood pressure) and dilating airways. This is then followed by an oral antihistamine. People who suffer reactions of this type require emergency medical treatment, even after they have had an injection of epinephrine.

A **delayed hypersensitivity** reaction refers to an allergy that usually takes several days to appear. A familiar example is **contact dermatitis**. This refers to itching, redness, and swelling of skin caused by exposure to substances such as poison ivy, certain cosmetic chemicals, or some heavy metals (mercury and lead), which in the extracellular matrix. In addition, histamine may make the affected area feel itchy. Thus, histamine is largely responsible for the typical symptoms of anaphylaxis: a runny nose, hives, and watery eyes. Treatment usually includes administration of an antihistamine agent, which blocks histamine production or release.

Figure 9.1 Poison ivy leaves contain oils that cause an allergic reaction in some people. When the body is exposed to these oils, white blood cells called lymphocytes release chemicals that cause itching, redness, and swelling. This response is known as contact dermatitis.

provoke an allergic response in sensitive individuals (Figure 9.1). In this case, white blood cells known as lymphocytes inappropriately respond by releasing chemicals called *lymphokines*. Thus, antihistamines are not helpful in treating a delayed hypersensitivity. Instead, corticosteroid drugs are used. They provide relief by inhibiting the release of lymphokines.

INFECTIONS

Skin infections can be caused by bacteria, viruses, and fungi. A fairly common bacterial infection is **impetigo**, which is characterized by pink, water-filled, raised lesions that develop a yellow crust and eventually rupture. Impetigo is highly contagious and relatively common in young, school-aged children. A bacterial infection of a hair follicle and/or sebaceous glands can cause a **boil**. The infection can spread to the underlying hypodermis and cause a fair amount of discomfort. Two common fungal skin infections are **athlete's foot** and ringworm (Figure 9.2). Both are characterized by an itchy, red, peeling condition and are treated with antifungal agents.

Cold sores, or fever blisters, are small, fluid-filled blisters that itch and sting. They are caused by a *Herpes simplex* viral infection. The virus localizes in a cutaneous nerve, where it remains dormant until activated by emotional upset, fever, or ultraviolet radiation. Cold sores usually occur around the lips and in the soft, moist lining of the mouth. A related *Herpes simplex* virus causes genital herpes, a sexually transmitted disease that can also be spread to the mouth. (Note that measles and mononucleosis are both caused by different types of *Herpes simplex* viruses). As stated previously, human papilloma viruses stimulate rapid cell division in the stratum basale, which leads to the formation of a wart.

ACNE

About four out of five teenagers are afflicted with acne, a skin condition that affects hair follicles and sebaceous glands (Figure 9.3). For this reason, acne occurs on areas of the body where oil glands are largest and most numerous: the face, chest, upper back, and shoulders. Adolescents are most prone to acne because sebaceous glands increase both in size and in production of sebum in response to increasing levels of androgens (male sex hormones). Androgens are secreted by endocrine cells in the testes, ovaries, and adrenal glands. Because

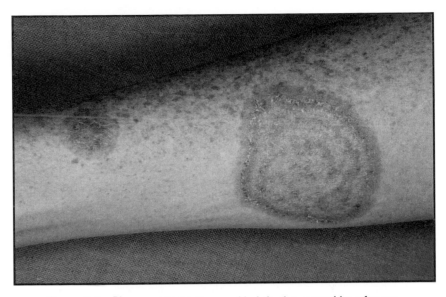

Figure 9.2 Ringworm is a common skin infection caused by a fungus, not a worm. The fungus can cause a circular, red, itchy rash. The condition is treated with antifungal medications.

males generally have higher levels of circulating androgens than females, their acne is typically more severe. However, acne can flare up in women around the time of menstruation, when levels of the hormone progesterone have increased following ovulation.

Acne is essentially an inflammation that results when sebum and dead cells clog the duct of a sebaceous gland in a hair follicle. A follicle obstructed in this manner forms a *whitehead*. Sometimes, the sebum in plugged follicles oxidizes and mixes with melanin, causing a *blackhead* to form. The next stage of acne is typically a red, raised bump, often with a white dot of pus in the center. The bump appears when obstructed follicles rupture and spew their contents into the surrounding epidermis. This small infection (a pimple) usually heals in a week or two. However, in severe cases of acne, the rupture of plugged follicles can produce large cysts that extend into the dermis, which may leave a scar when healed.

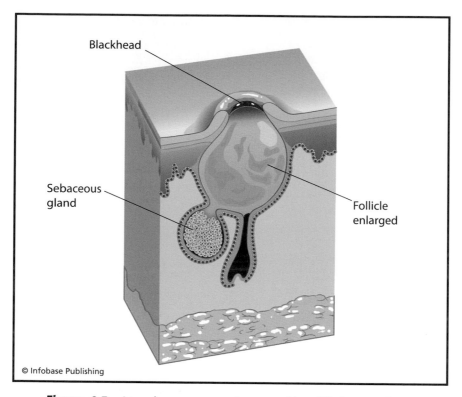

Blackhead

Sebaceous
gland

Follicle
enlarged

© Infobase Publishing

Figure 9.3 Acne is a common teenage skin affliction. During adolescence, the body increases its production of sebum. This excess sebum can mix with dead cells and become trapped in a hair follicle. When the sebum oxidizes and mixes with melanin, a blackhead will form, as is shown in this diagram.

Contrary to popular belief, acne is not caused by eating certain foods, such as chocolate, pizza, and potato chips (although there are other legitimate health concerns with a diet high in saturated fat and low in fruits and vegetables). In addition, because follicles plug from below, dirt or oil on the skin surface is not responsible for causing acne. Nonetheless, washing the face with warm water will help open plugged follicles. It also turns out that acne has a genetic link. In other words, individuals are more likely to develop acne if their parents had this problem. Finally, acne is more likely to flare up during times of stress, presumably due to stress-induced changes in hormone levels.

Treatment for acne includes some topical agents, which are applied directly to the skin. For example, benzoyl peroxide is commonly used because it is a powerful antibacterial agent that kills bacteria living in hair follicles. Severe cases of acne may require oral medication, such as an antibiotic agent that inhibits bacteria that inhabit follicles.

SKIN CANCER

Skin cancer is the most common type of cancer. An important risk factor in developing this disease is overexposure to ultra-violet rays in sunlight. This form of radiation can suppress the immune system, making it more difficult for the body to fight the formation of cancer cells. Ultraviolet radiation also has sufficient energy to alter the structure of DNA, thereby caus-ing mutations. In addition, some cases of chronic irritation of the skin by infections, chemicals, or physical trauma may be risk factors for skin cancer.

Cancer arising in epithelial tissue is called a **carcinoma**, and it accounts for over 90% of all cancers. These cancers occur most frequently in light-skinned people over the age of forty, especially in those who have been exposed to sunlight on a regular basis, such as farmers, construction workers, and sun-bathers. In addition, episodes of severe sunburn during child-hood appear to predispose individuals to develop skin cancer many years later. That is why it is important to practice cancer prevention at an early age.

The least malignant and most common form of skin cancer is **basal cell carcinoma**. In fact, over 30% of Caucasians develop this type of cancer. Basal cell carcinoma originates in the actively dividing cells of the stratum basale, usually in sun-exposed areas of the face. Although it can invade the dermis and hypodermis, it is a slow-growing cancer. Surgical removal is prescribed, and usually provides a full cure if caught before the cancer has spread. **Squamous cell carcinoma** arises from the keratinocytes of the stratum spinosum, usually on the scalp, ears, lower lip, and hands. It tends to grow rapidly and will metastasize if not removed. However, if caught early and surgically removed, the chance of a complete cure is good.

Cancer of melanocytes is called **melanoma**. This is the most dangerous form of skin cancer. Melanomas can appear spontaneously or develop from a preexisting mole. They form most often in light-skinned people who tend to burn rather than tan. In addition, short, intermittent exposure to high-intensity sunlight appears to initiate these growths. For instance, melanomas are less common in people who stay indoors most of the time, but more common in those who occasionally sustain blistering sunburns. This form of cancer metastasizes quickly into lymph and blood vessels. Therefore, the key to survival is early detection. The usual treatment is surgical removal and chemotherapy.

To reduce the chances of developing skin cancer, avoid excessive exposure to ultraviolet light, especially during the midday hours when the sun's rays are at their strongest. Wearing a wide-brimmed hat will help keep sunlight off your face and neck. In addition, use sunscreens that have a sun protection factor (SPF) of at least 15. Keep in mind that ultraviolet rays can pass through clouds, penetrate water up to about 3 feet (about 1 m), and reflect off surfaces such as sand and a patio deck. Further, tanning salons also expose individuals to ultraviolet light, especially to a form of ultraviolet light called UV-A, which has been shown to suppress the immune system. Finally, examine skin regularly for abnormal growths, particularly those that change color, shape, or surface texture.

BURNS

A *burn* refers to tissue damage caused by intense heat, electricity, radiation, or certain chemicals, all of which denature proteins, thereby leading to cell death. The activity of a protein, such as an enzyme, depends on its three-dimensional shape, which is typically held in place by hydrogen bonds. However, these bonds are relatively weak and easily broken by excessive heat. In **denaturation**, the hydrogen bonds are broken, causing the protein to unfold and lose its ability to function. A protein is said to be *denatured* when this occurs.

Burns are classified according to the depth to which the tissue damage penetrates (Figure 9.4). **First-degree burns** are confined to the upper layers of epidermis. The affected area becomes red and swollen. These burns are generally not serious and heal in a few days. A mild sunburn is an example of a first-degree burn.

Damage from a **second-degree burn** extends through the epidermis into the upper region of the dermis. As a result, blisters appear. Because sufficient epithelium remains intact, regeneration of skin can occur, and no permanent scars will result if care is taken to prevent infection. **Third-degree burns**, on the other hand, extend all the way through the epidermis and dermis into underlying subcutaneous tissues. The burned area appears blanched or blackened. Strangely enough, third-degree burns do not hurt initially because nerve endings in the dermis are destroyed. Unfortunately, regeneration of skin is

YOUR HEALTH: SKIN CANCER

The American Cancer Society suggests the **ABCD rule** when checking for skin cancer:

- A: *asymmetry*, because most melanomas are irregular in shape
- B: *border*, because melanomas often have diffuse, unclear borders
- C: *color*, because melanomas usually have a mottled appearance, containing brown, black, red, white, or blue colors
- D: *diameter*, because skin growths with a diameter of more than about 0.2 inches (5 mm) are life threatening

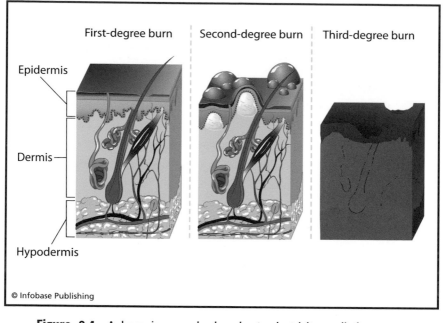

First-degree burn Second-degree burn Third-degree burn

Epidermis

Dermis

Hypodermis

© Infobase Publishing

Figure 9.4 A burn is caused when heat, electricity, radiation, or caustic chemicals denature proteins and cause cell death. First-degree burns occur when only the epidermis, is affected. Burns that penetrate the dermis are considered second-degree burns. The burn can heal completely, but some scarring may occur. Third-degree burns occur when cells in the subcutaneous tissue (hypodermis) are affected. Hair follicles and nerve endings may be damaged, and skin regeneration is not usually likely.

not possible. Therefore, skin grafting is necessary to cover the underlying exposed tissues.

Severe burns, particularly those covering large portions of the body, are life threatening. The immediate concern is loss of body fluids containing proteins and electrolytes (salts), resulting from the loss of an effective waterproof barrier. Sufficient dehydration and electrolyte imbalance may lead to shutdown of the kidneys and also to circulatory shock from inadequate circulation of blood due to a low fluid volume. In this case, fluids must be replaced immediately. In addition, many calories are needed to replace those lost as proteins. Consequently, severe burn patients are given supplementary nutrients through gastric tubes and intravenous lines.

Once fluid volumes have been restored, infection becomes the most important threat. In fact, infection is the leading cause of death in burn victims. Burned skin is sterile for about 24 hours. However, soon thereafter, opportunistic bacteria and fungi easily invade areas where skin has been destroyed. The situation is exacerbated by depression of the immune system, which usually occurs within one or two days after a severe burn.

BIRTHMARKS

It is not uncommon for people to be born with red birthmarks called **port wine stains**. Their cause is not known; however, they contain an abnormally dense collection of dermal blood vessels, usually on the face or neck. As the body grows, so does the birthmark. In some cases, the mark darkens with age, and it may also develop a bumpy texture due to nodules of blood vessels. Although there is no known health risk associated with birthmarks, there may be a psychological aspect. Laser therapy is often used to remove these blemishes.

ROSACEA

Rosacea is characterized by engorgement of blood vessels, especially of the cheeks and nose. The disorder causes persistent flushing of facial skin, which appears red and inflamed and is also marked with whitehead-like bumps and spidery blood vessels. It tends to strike most often in people between the ages of 30 and 50. Although it is more common in women, its symptoms are more acute in men. Untreated, rosacea gradually and painlessly disfigures the skin with patches of swollen veins and clusters of pustules. Those afflicted with rosacea are often given antibiotics. These individuals may also seek laser treatment to destroy swollen blood vessels.

The exact cause of rosacea is unknown. Alcohol consumption and poor hygiene are no longer believed to cause rosacea;

however, drinking alcohol, eating spicy foods, emotional stress, and exposure to sunlight may trigger facial flushing, thereby causing symptoms to become worse. Tiny mites (*Demodex folliculorum*) that normally live on the skin may play a role in this disease because people with rosacea tend to have more of these mites on their faces than those who do not have the disease. There may also be a link between rosacea and skin infection with *Helicobacter pylori*, a bacterium that causes stomach ulcers.

BEDSORES

Long-term restriction of blood flow to the skin will result in death of cells. If the restriction is severe enough, skin ulcers, or bedsores, will form. This problem is most common in bed-ridden individuals who are not turned regularly or who are repeatedly dragged across a bed. The weight of body parts puts pressure on the skin, especially over bony projections. Because this restricts blood supply, the skin becomes blanched (pale) at these locations. If the situation is not corrected, cells will eventually die, leading to breaks in the skin at compressed sites. Permanent damage to the superficial blood flow eventually results in degeneration and ulceration of skin.

CONNECTIONS

The most common skin disorders result from bacterial (impetigo, acne, boils), viral (cold sore, wart), and fungal (ringworm) infections and from allergies. An allergy occurs when a normally harmless substance, an allergen, evokes an inappropriate immune response. An immediate hypersensitivity refers to a response within minutes after contacting an allergen and is caused by inappropriate release of histamine from mast cells. Contact dermatitis, such as from poison ivy, results from release of lymphokines from lymphocytes.

Skin cancer is the most common type of cancer. An important risk factor in developing this disease is overexposure to ultraviolet rays in sunlight. Cancer arising in epithelial tissue is called a carcinoma, and it accounts for over 90% of all cancers. The least malignant and most common form of skin cancer is basal cell carcinoma. Squamous cell carcinoma arises from the keratinocytes of the stratum spinosum, usually on the scalp, ears, lower lip, and hands. Cancer of melanocytes is called melanoma. This is the most dangerous form of skin cancer.

A burn refers to tissue damage caused by intense heat, electricity, radiation, or certain chemicals, all of which denature proteins, thereby leading to cell death. First-degree burns are confined to the upper layers of epidermis, whereas second-degree burns extend through the epidermis into the upper region of the dermis. Third-degree burns extend all the way through the epidermis and dermis, into underlying subcutaneous tissues. Severe burns can be life threatening because of resulting fluid loss and infection.

Appendix: Conversion Chart

Unit (metric)		Metric to English	English to Metric	
LENGTH				
Kilometer	km	1 km 0.62 mile (mi)	1 mile (mi)	1.609 km
Meter	m	1 m 3.28 feet (ft)	1 foot (ft)	0.305 m
Centimeter	cm	1 cm 0.394 inches (in)	1 inch (in)	2.54 cm
Millimeter	mm	1 mm 0.039 inches (in)	1 inch (in)	25.4 mm
Micrometer	μm	1-millionth meter		
WEIGHT (MASS)				
Kilogram	kg	1 kg 2.2 pounds (lbs)	1 pound (lbs)	0.454 kg
Gram	g	1 g 0.035 ounces (oz)	1 ounce (oz)	28.35 g
Milligram	mg	1 mg 0.000035 ounces (oz)		
Microgram	μg	1-millionth gram		
VOLUME				
Liter	L	1 L 1.06 quarts	1 gallon (gal)	3.785 L
			1 quart (qt)	0.94 L
			1 pint (pt)	0.47 L
Milliliter	mL or cc	1 mL 0.034 fluid ounce (fl oz)	1 fluid ounce (fl oz)	29.57 mL
Microliter	μL	1-millionth liter		
TEMPERATURE				
		°F = 9/5°C + 32	°C = 5/9 (°F − 32)	

Glossary

ABCD rule   A list of suggestions provided by the American Cancer Society when checking for skin cancer.

Acne   An inflammation caused by sebum and dead cells clogging a sebaceous gland duct.

Active transport   A membrane transport process that requires cell expenditure of ATP; usually involves solute pumping against a concentration gradient.

Adenosine triphosphate (ATP)   An organic molecule that is the main source of immediate energy for use by cells.

Adipose tissue   Loose connective tissue modified to store fat.

Albinism   An inherited disorder characterized by the inability of melanocytes to produce melanin.

Allergy   An inappropriate and overzealous immune response to a substance (allergen) that otherwise would be harmless.

Anaphase   The stage of mitosis in which full sets of daughter chromosomes move to opposite spindle poles.

Anucleate   A cell without a nucleus.

Apical surface   The outer surface of epithelial tissue that is exposed to the external environment or a body cavity.

Apocrine gland   A type of sweat gland that produces a secretion of water, salts, proteins, and fatty acids in response to fear, anger, or sexual excitement.

Apoptosis   Programmed cell death, characterized by destruction of chromatin and the nuclear envelope and cell shrinkage.

Areolar tissue   Loose connective tissue found throughout the body; acts as packing material and glue.

Arrector pili muscles   Tiny, smooth muscles attached to hair follicles; they contract in response to cold or fear, causing goose bumps.

Athlete's foot   A fungal infection of the feet characterized by itchy, red, peeling skin.

Basal cell carcinoma   The most common form of skin cancer; it originates in the actively dividing cells of the stratum basale, usually in sun-exposed areas of the face.

Basal lamina   The nonliving supporting layer of the basement membrane secreted by epithelial cells.

Basal surface   The inner surface of epithelial tissue that is anchored to the basement membrane.

Basement membrane   Extracellular material consisting of the basal lamina secreted by epithelial cells and the reticular lamina secreted by connective tissue cells.

Basophil   A type of white blood cell that releases histamine.

Benign   A term referring to tumors that lack the ability to invade surrounding tissues; not malignant.

Biconcave   Having two depressions, one on either side of a disk-shaped cell.

Bilayer   Having two layers, usually referring to the phospholipid layers of a cell membrane.

Boil   A bacterial infection of a hair follicle and/or sebaceous gland.

Carbohydrate   An organic compound composed of carbon, hydrogen, and oxygen; includes sugars, glycogen, and starch.

Cancer   A malignant mass of altered cells that divide abnormally and are capable of spreading to other body parts.

Carcinogen   A chemical or other agent that causes cancer.

Carcinoma   A tumor that arises in epithelial tissue.

Cardiac muscle   A contractile tissue found only in the heart wall.

Carotene   A yellow-orange pigment found in many foods; can accumulate in the stratum corneum of skin.

Carrier   A membrane protein that moves substances by facilitated diffusion.

Cartilage   Connective tissue composed of chondrocytes and a solid, flexible matrix.

Cell   The smallest unit having the properties of life.

Cell adhesion molecule   A membrane protein that links cells together.

Cell-cell recognition   The ability of the receptors of one cell type to recognize glycoproteins of another cell.

Cell cycle   The periodic division of cell nucleus and cytoplasm to form two daughter cells.

Cell theory   The concepts that all organisms consist of one or more cells; the cell is the smallest unit with the capacity of independent life, and all cells arise from preexisting cells.

Centriole   A small structure that gives rise to microtubules of cilia, flagella, and spindle fibers.

Cerumen   A sticky, bitter substance; also called earwax.

Ceruminous gland   A modified apocrine gland found in the lining of the external ear; produces earwax.

Channel   A term use to describe a membrane protein that forms an aqueous pore in a membrane through which ions can traverse.

Cholesterol   A type of lipid found in most animal fats and cell membranes; synthesized by the liver.

Chondrocyte   A mature connective tissue cell type that forms cartilage.

Chromatin   DNA and associated proteins.

Chromosome   Elongated bodies of tightly coiled chromatin that are visible during cell division.

Cilia   Tiny, motile, hairlike projections on a cell surface.

Cleavage furrow   An indentation of the cell membrane during cytokinesis; caused by contraction of a ring of microfilaments over the midline of the spindle.

Cold sore   Small, fluid-filled blisters that itch and sting; infection caused by a *Herpes simplex* virus.

Collagen   The most abundant protein fiber found in the extracellular matrix of connective tissue.

Columnar   Cylindrical or shaped like a column.

Concentration gradient   The difference in concentration of a particular substance between two different areas.

Connective tissue   A primary tissue form that includes bone, cartilage, adipose tissue, and blood.

Contact dermatitis   Itching, redness, and swelling of skin caused by exposure to substances that provoke an allergic response in sensitive individuals.

Cuboidal   Cubelike in shape.

Cutaneous membrane   A term used to describe skin; however, the term is misleading because skin is actually an organ.

Cuticle   The fold of skin projecting over the proximal end of nails.

Cyanosis   A bluish skin color resulting from poorly oxygenated hemoglobin.

Cytokinesis   The division of the cytoplasm, usually following nuclear division.

Cytoplasm   The cellular material surrounding the nucleus and enclosed by the plasma membrane.

Cytoskeleton   A dynamic and elaborate series of internal rods in the cytosol; they support cellular structures, help maintain cell shape, and provide the machinery to generate various cell movements.

Cytosol   The viscous, semitransparent fluid substance of the cytoplasm in which other structures are suspended.

Delayed hypersensitivity   An allergic reaction that usually occurs in sensitized individuals 24 to 48 hours after exposure to an allergen; mainly caused by lymphokine released from lymphocytes.

Denaturation   The unfolding of proteins, causing them to lose their specific three-dimensional shape; denatured proteins are nonfunctional.

Dermis   The layer of skin beneath the epidermis; composed of dense and loose connective tissue.

Differentiation   The development of specific characteristics in cells as a result of the expression of some genes and repression of others.

Diffusion   The spreading of particles as a result of kinetic energy from an area of higher concentration to an area of lower concentration.

DNA (deoxyribonucleic acid)   The carrier of hereditary information; a macromolecule in the form of a double helix and found in the cell nucleus; DNA and histone proteins make up the chromosomes.

Eccrine gland   Abundant sweat glands whose secretion is primarily used for temperature regulation.

Elastic cartilage   A type of cartilage containing an abundance of elastic fibers, which gives the tissue a great tolerance for repeated bending.

Elastic fiber   Long, thin protein fibers found in the extracellular matrix of connective tissue.

Elastin   A resilient, rubberlike protein secreted into the extracellular space by connective tissue cells.

Electromagnetic radiation   A form of energy that travels in waves and is capable of moving through a vacuum; includes X-rays, ultraviolet rays, visible light, infrared radiation, and radio waves.

Electron microscope   A device that uses a beam of electrons focused by electromagnets to magnify the image of a specimen.

Element   A fundamental form of matter that cannot normally be broken down into another substance by chemical means.

Endocrine glands   Ductless glands that secrete hormones into the bloodstream.

Endocytosis   A method of vesicular transport by which fairly large extracellular substances enter cells.

Endoplasmic reticulum   An organelle composed of a membranous network of tubular and saclike channels in the cytoplasm; modifies newly formed proteins and synthesizes lipids.

Enzyme   A biological molecule, usually a protein, that increases the rate of a chemical reaction in cells.

Epidermis   The outer layer of skin composed of keratinized, stratified squamous epithelium.

Epithelial tissue (epithelium)   The tissue that covers the body surface and lines its internal cavities, tubes, and organs, and forms glands.

Equilibrium   The point at which there is no net change in a chemical reaction or net movement by diffusion.

Erythrocyte   Red blood cell.

Exocrine gland   A gland that secretes its products into a duct or tube.

Exocytosis   A method of vesicular transport by which fairly large intracellular substances exit cells.

Extracellular matrix   Nonliving material secreted by connective tissue cells; it contains protein fibers and ground substance and separates living cells.

Facilitated diffusion   A passive transport mechanism that uses a protein carrier.

Fatty acid A linear chain of carbon and hydrogen atoms with an organic acid group at one end.

Fibroblast   An actively dividing cell that forms loose and dense connective tissues.

Fibrocartilage   A type of cartilage found in vertebral discs and the knee joint.

Filtration   Movement of water and solute particles through membranes as a result of hydrostatic pressure.

First-degree burn   A burn confined to the upper layers of epidermis, such as a mild sunburn.

Flagella   Long, whiplike extensions on a cell surface; in humans, found only on sperm cells.

Fluid-mosaic model   The idea that cell membranes consist of a phospholipid bilayer in which proteins are dispersed.

Free radical   Highly reactive chemicals containing unpaired electrons; free radicals can alter the structure of proteins, lipids, and nucleic acids.

Gamete   A germ cell (sperm or ovum) that contains half the normal number of chromosomes.

Gene   A unit of hereditary information found in the DNA of chromosomes.

Glycocalyx   A layer of glycoproteins that act as biological markers; found on the outside of plasma membranes.

Glycolipid   A lipid molecule with one or more sugars covalently bonded to it.

Glycoprotein   A protein molecule with one or more sugars covalently bonded to it.

Golgi apparatus   A membranous organelle that sorts and packages proteins for export from the cell.

Ground substance   Nonliving intercellular material of the extracellular matrix that is secreted by connective tissue cells.

Hair bulb   The deep, expanded end of a hair follicle.

Hair follicle   A compound structure of epidermis and dermis that surrounds a hair root and forms new hair.

Hair root plexus   A knot of sensory nerve endings that wraps around each hair bulb.

Hemoglobin   The iron-containing pigment in red blood cells; it carries oxygen from the lungs to the body tissues and some carbon dioxide from the body cells to the lungs.

Histamine   A chemical released by mast cells in an allergic reaction; causes vasodilation and increased vascular permeability.

Histology   The study of tissues and their microscopic structure.

Homeostasis   The maintenance of a relatively stable internal environment of the body resulting from the activity of organ systems.

Hyaline cartilage   The most abundant type of cartilage; provides firm support with some flexibility.

Hydrophilic   A polar substance that dissolves in water.

Hydrophobic   A nonpolar substance that does not dissolve in water.

Hydrostatic pressure   The pressure exerted by the volume of a fluid against a wall that encloses the fluid, such as the pressure generated on the walls of blood vessels when the heart contracts.

Hypertonic solution   A solution that has a higher osmotic pressure than body fluids and therefore causes cells to lose water and shrink.

Hypotonic solution   A solution that has a lower osmotic pressure than body fluids and therefore causes cells to gain water and swell.

Impetigo   A fairly common, highly contagious bacterial infection characterized by pink, water-filled raised skin lesions that develop a yellow crust and eventually rupture.

Immediate hypersensitivity   An allergic reaction that usually occurs within seconds or minutes of exposure to an allergen, mainly caused by histamine released from mast cells.

Inclusion   A collection of chemical substances in cells, such as stored nutrients or cell products.

Inorganic compounds   Substances that do not contain carbon and hydrogen, such as water, salts, minerals, and many acids and bases; not organic.

Integral protein   A protein that is embedded within the lipid bilayer of a cell membrane.

Integumentary system   Skin and its derivatives; forms the outer protective layer of the body.

Intermediate filament   A cytoskeletal element that mechanically strengthens some cells.

Interphase   The interval between nuclear divisions during which a cell increases in mass and duplicates its chromosomes.

Isotonic solution   A fluid that has the same osmotic pressure as body fluids.

Jaundice   A yellowish skin color resulting from excess bile pigments in the blood.

Keratin   A tough, fibrous protein found in keratinocytes of the epidermis, hair, and nails.

Keratinocyte   The most common cell type in the epidermis; these cells enable the skin to act as a protective barrier.

Kinetic energy   The energy of motion.

Lacuna (plural: lacunae)   A small cavity in bone or cartilage; occupied by osteocyte or chondrocyte, respectively.

Langerhans cell   A type of macrophage found in the epidermis that ingests foreign particles.

Lanugo   The soft, fine hair that covers a fetus.

Leukocyte   A white blood cell.

Light microscope   A device that uses optical lenses to refract and focus a beam of light in order to magnify the image of a specimen.

Lipid   An organic compound made up of carbon, hydrogen, and oxygen that is insoluble in water; a fat.

Lunula   The whitish, crescent-shaped area at the base of a nail.

Lysosome   A vesicle that originates from the Golgi apparatus and contains digestive enzymes.

Malignant   A term referring to tumors that can spread and invade surrounding tissues.

Major elements   A group of four elements (carbon, hydrogen, oxygen, and nitrogen) that compose over 95% of the human body.

Male pattern baldness   A genetically determined, sex-influenced loss of hair.

Malignant   A type of tumor capable of spreading by metastasis to invade surrounding tissues; cancerous.

Mammary gland   Modified sweat glands, specialized to secrete milk.

Mast cell   A type of white blood cell capable of releasing histamine and other inflammatory factors.

Matrix   An actively dividing area of a follicle that forms hair.

Meiosis   A type of cell division that decreases the number of chromosomes to half in developing sperm and eggs; produces four daughter cells.

Melanin   A dark pigment produced by melanocytes that gives color to skin and hair.

Melanocyte   An epidermal skin cell that synthesizes and releases melanin.

Melanoma   A cancer of melanocytes.

Merkel cell   Sensory structure for touch found in the epidermis of skin.

Metabolism   The sum total of all the chemical reactions in the body.

Metaphase   The stage of mitosis in which all the duplicated chromosomes line up at the equator of a cell.

Metastasis   The spread of cancer from one body part to another not directly connected.

Microfilament   A cytoskeletal element involved in cell movement and maintenance of shape.

Micrometer   A unit of measurement equivalent to one-millionth of a meter.

Microtubule   A cytoskeletal element that plays a role in cell shape, growth, and motion.

Microvilli   Tiny, fingerlike projections on the apical surface of some epithelial cells; increase surface area.

Mitochondria   The organelles responsible for production of ATP.

Mitosis   Nuclear division that results in an equal distribution of identical genetic material to each daughter cell.

Muscle tissue   A tissue capable of generating force by contracting.

Mutagen   A substance or agent that can cause a change in the DNA base sequence.

Myelin sheath   An insulating layer around the axons of some neurons; formed by neuroglia.

Nail bed   The layer of epithelium under a nail that is continuous with the stratum basale of skin.

Nanometer   One-billionth of a meter.

Necrosis   The death of a cell or group of cells due to injury or disease.

Nervous tissue   A tissue type that includes neurons and neuroglia.

Neuroglia   Nervous system cells that support, protect, and insulate neurons.

Neurons   Nervous system cells capable of generating and conducting impulses.

Nonpolar (molecules)   Molecules in which the positive and negative charge centers are not separated so that there are no positive and negative regions on the molecule.

Nuclear envelope   A double-membrane barrier surrounding the nucleus.

Nuclear pore   A channel in the nuclear envelope that is permeable to water and solutes and regulates the transport of ribosomal subunits.

Nucleic acid   A class of organic molecules that includes DNA and RNA.

Nucleolus (plural: nucleoli)   A dense, spherical structure in the nucleus that is an assembly site for ribosomal subunits.

Nucleoplasm   The gel-like, fluid portion of a nucleus enclosed by the nuclear envelope; contains dissolved salts and nutrients.

Nucleus   The control center of the cell; contains the genetic material (DNA) and separates DNA from the cytoplasm.

Oncogene   Any gene having the potential to induce formation of cancer by stimulating cell division.

Organ A structure made up of two or more kinds of tissue and adapted to carry out a specific function (e.g., the kidney).

Organelle   A small cellular structure in the cytoplasm that performs specific functions for the cell as a whole.

Organic compounds   Type of compounds containing carbon and hydrogen, such as proteins, lipids, and carbohydrates.

Osmosis   Diffusion of water through a selectively permeable membrane down its concentration gradient from a region of higher water (lower solute) concentration to one of lower water (higher solute) concentration.

Osmotic pressure   The pressure necessary to stop the flow of water by osmosis.

Osteocyte   A mature bone cell.

Osteon   A microscopic structure of compact bone consisting of an elongated cylinder composed of concentric rings of extracellular matrix called lamellae.

Papilla   The nipple-like region of dermis that nourishes a growing hair.

Papillary layer   The thinner outer layer of the dermis composed of loose connective tissue.

Passive transport   A membrane transport process that does not require cellular energy.

Peripheral protein   A protein located on the outer or inner surface of a cell membrane.

Peroxisome   A vesicle that detoxifies harmful substances such as free radicals.

Phagocytosis   A kind of endocystosis in which cells surround and engulf solid particles.

Phosphate group   A group of atoms consisting of one phosphorous and four oxygen atoms.

Phospholipid   A lipid consisting of two fatty acid chains and a phosphate group bonded to a 3-carbon glycerol molecule; major component of cell membranes.

Pinocytosis   A vesicular transport of fluid containing dissolved substances; "cell drinking."

Plasma   The liquid portion of blood composed of water and various solutes.

Plasma membrane   The outermost structure of a cell; forms a structural and functional boundary between the cytoplasm and the outside environment.

Platelets   Cell fragments that both release substances needed for blood clotting and help to plug a wound.

Polar (molecules)   Molecules in which the positive and negative charge centers are separated so that the molecule has separate regions with slight positive and negative charge.

Port wine stain   A red birthmark that contains an abnormally dense collection of dermal blood vessels, usually on the face or neck.

Prophase   The first phase in mitosis in which the duplicated genetic material condenses into chromosomes.

Protein   A complex organic molecule made up of a specific sequence of amino acids.

Pseudostratified epithelium   A single layer of epithelial cells that has a multilayered appearance.

Receptor   A protein with binding sites that interact with specific molecules.

Resolution   The ability to show as separate two points that are close together.

Reticular lamina   A layer of extracellular material that is a major component of the basement membrane; secreted by connective tissue cells.

Reticular layer   The thicker inner layer of the dermis; composed of dense connective tissue.

Ribosome   A nonmembranous organelle that is the site of protein synthesis.

RNA (ribonucleic acid)   Single-stranded macromolecules that carry out DNA's instructions for protein synthesis.

Rosacea   A flushing of facial skin characterized by engorgement of blood vessels, especially of the cheeks and nose.

Scanning electron microscope   An electron microscope that produces an image of the specimen surface by scanning the surface with a beam of electrons.

Sebaceous gland   An oil gland that secretes sebum, usually into a hair follicle.

Sebum   Oily substance made of fats, cholesterol, protein, and salts that lubricates hair and skin.

Second-degree burn   A burn with damage extending through the epidermis into the upper region of the dermis.

Selectively permeable   The capacity of cell membranes to let some substances through but not others.

Semipermeable   See *Selectively permeable.*

Simple diffusion   The unassisted transport of lipid-soluble substances across a cell membrane down their concentration gradients.

Simple epithelium   Epithelial cells arranged in a single layer.

Skeletal muscle   Voluntary, striated muscle connected to bones; responsible for most body movements.

Smooth muscle   Nonstriated muscle not under voluntary control; found in hollow organs and around blood vessels.

Solute   Any substance dissolved in a solution.

Solute pump   A protein carrier that mediates active transport of solutes across a cell membrane against their concentration gradients.

Solvent   Any fluid, such as water, in which one or more substances is dissolved.

Spontaneous generation   The concept that living organisms arise spontaneously from nonliving material, such as garbage.

Squamous   Flat or scalelike.

Squamous cell carcinoma   A type of skin cancer that arises from the keratinocytes of the stratum spinosum, usually on the scalp, ears, lower lip, and hands.

Stain   A dye used to increase contrast between cell structures for light microscopy.

Stem cell   An undifferentiated cell possessing the potential to become any cell type.

Stratified epithelium   A type of epithelium in which the cells are arranged in multiple layers.

Stratum basale   The deepest layer of the epidermis, with cells that are capable of active cell division.

Stratum corneum   The outer layer of the epidermis; composed of flattened, dead, keratinized cells.

Stratum granulosum   The layer of the epidermis composed of flattened cells containing keratohyalin, a substance that contributes to the formation of keratin.

Stratum lucidum   A layer of flattened, dead cells found in thick skin, as on the palms of the hands and soles of the feet.

Stratum spinosum   The second-deepest layer of the epidermis; contains cuboidal keratinocytes and scattered melanin granules and Langerhans cells.

Subcutaneous tissue   A layer of connective tissue below the skin; it anchors the skin, stores fat, and acts as thermal and mechanical insulation.

Sweat glands   Epidermal glands that produce sweat; also called *sudoriferous glands*.

Telomeres   Special caps on the end of chromosomes that protect them from fraying or fusing with other chromosomes.

Telophase   The final phase of mitosis that begins when the chromosomes have migrated to the poles of the cells and ends with the formation of two complete nuclei.

Terminal hair   Thick, strong hair, such as that of the scalp, eyebrows and eyelashes.

Third-degree burn   A burn that extends all the way through the epidermis and dermis into underlying subcutaneous tissues.

Tissue   A group of similar cells and intercellular substances specialized to perform a specific function.

Trace element   An element that makes up less than 0.01% of body weight.

Transitional epithelium   A type of epithelium that lines organs and is subject to considerable stretching.

Transmission electron microscope   An electron microscope that uses electromagnets to focus a beam of electrons that pass through a very thin specimen to reveal internal structure.

Tumor   A tissue mass composed of cells that are dividing at an abnormally high rate; can be cancerous.

Tumor-suppressor gene   A gene that checks for proper DNA duplication; initiates apoptosis when damage to DNA is not reparable.

Vasoconstriction   A narrowing of blood vessels due to contraction of smooth muscle in vessel walls.

Vasodilation   A widening of blood vessels due to relaxation of the smooth muscle in vessel walls.

Vellus hair   Soft, fine hair that persists throughout life and covers most of the body surface.

Vesicle   A small, fluid-filled membranous sac.

Vesicular transport   The movement of fairly large particles across cell membranes by enclosing them in vesicles; endocytosis and exocytosis.

Bibliography

Ackerman, M.J., and D.E. Clapham. "Ion Channels: Basic Science and Clinical Disease." *Mechanisms of Disease* 336 (1997): 1575–1586.

Alberts, B., A. Johnson, J. Lewis, M. Raff, D. Bray, K. Hopkins, and K. Roberts. *Essential Cell Biology.* 2nd ed. New York: Garland, 2003.

Alberts, B., A. Johnson, J. Lewis, M. Raff, K. Roberts, and P. Walter. *Molecular Biology of the Cell.* 5th ed. New York: Garland, 2002.

Appell, D. "Getting Under Your Skin." *Scientific American* 288 (2003): 18–20.

Ashcroft, F. *Ion Channels and Disease: Channelopathies.* New York: Academic Press, 2000.

Bayley, H. "Building Doors into Cells." *Scientific American* 277 (1997): 62–67.

Beardsley, T. "Getting Wired. New Observations May Show How Neurons Form Connections." *Scientific American* 280 (1999): 24–26.

———. "Stem Cells Come of Age." *Scientific American* 281 (1999): 30–31.

Boon, T. "Teaching the Immune System to Fight Cancer." *Scientific American* 263 (1993): 782–789.

Bray, D. *Cell Movements: From Molecules to Motility.* 2nd ed. New York: Routledge, 2000.

Bretscher, M.S. "The Molecules of the Cell Membrane." *Scientific American* 253 (1985): 100–108.

Byrne, J.H., and S.G. Schultz. *Introduction to Membrane Transport and Bioelectricity: Foundations of General Physiology and Electrochemical Signaling.* New York: Raven Press, 1994.

Campbell, N., and J.B. Reece. *Biology.* 7th ed. Benjamin Cummings, 2004.

Cavance, W.K., and R.L. White. "The Genetic Basis of Cancer." *Scientific American* 272 (1995): 72–79.

Chan, S., and E. Blackburn. "Telomeres and Telomerase." *Philosophical Transactions of the Royal Society of London B Biological Science* 359 (2004): 109–121.

Chiras, D.D. *Human Biology.* 5th ed. Jones & Bartlett, 2005.

Christensen, T., A. Moller-Larsen, and S. Haahr. "A Retroviral Implication in Multiple Sclerosis." *Trends in Microbiology* 2 (1994): 332–336.

Clark, D. *Molecular Biology Made Fun and Simple.* 3rd ed. Chache River Press, 2005.

Cooper, E.C., and L. Yeh Jan. "Ion Channel Genes and Human Neurological Disease: Recent Progress, Prospects, and Challenges." *Proceedings of the National Academy of Sciences* 96 (1999): 4759–4766.

Darnell, J., P. Matsudaira, L. Zipursky, H. Lodish, A. Berk, and D. Baltimore. *Molecular Cell Biology.* 4th ed. New York: Freeman, 1999.

Davidson, A., and B. Diamond. "Autoimmune Diseases." *New England Journal of Medicine* 345 (2001): 340–350.

Dhabhar, F. "Stress, Leukocyte Trafficking, and the Augmentation of Skin Immune Function." *Annals of the New York Academy of Sciences* 992 (2003): 205–217.

Donald, O., J. Kajistura, S. Chimenti, D. Bodine, A. Leri, and P. Anversa. "Bone Marrow Stem Cells Regenerate Infarcted Myocardium." *Pediatric Transplantation* 7 (2003): 86–88.

Duke, R.C., D.M. Ojcius, and J.D. Young. "Cell Suicide in Health and Disease." *Scientific American* 275 (1996): 80–87.

Dyer, C. "The Structure and Function of Myelin: From Inert Membrane to Perfusion Pump." *Neurochemical Research* 27 (2002): 1279–1292.

Engleman, D. "Membranes Are More Mosaic than Fluid." *Nature* 438 (2005): 578–580.

Ezzell, C. "Starving Tumors of Their Lifeblood." *Scientific American* 279 (1998): 33–34.

Feldman, M., and L. Eisenbach. "What Makes a Tumor Cell Metastatic?" *Scientific American* 259 (1988): 60–65.

Fischetti, M. "Tan or Burn." *Scientific American* 285 (2001): 90–91.

Golde, D.W. "The Stem Cell." *Scientific American* 265 (1991): 86–93.

Goodsell, D.S. "Inside a Living Cell." *Trends in Biochemistry* 16 (1991): 203–206.

Greider, C.W., and E.H. Blackburn. "Telomeres, Telomerase, and Cancer." *Scientific American* 274 (1996): 92–97.

Hall, B. *Bones and Cartilage*. New York: Academic Press, 2005.

Hille, B. *Ionic Channels of Excitable Membranes*. 3rd ed. Sunderland, Mass.: Sinauer, 2001.

Ingber, D.E. "The Architecture of Life." *Scientific American* 278 (1998): 48–57.

Jablonksi, N.G., and G. Chaplin. "Skin Deep." *Scientific American* 287 (2002): 74–81.

Johnson, M.D. *Human Biology: Concepts and Current Issues*. 3rd ed. San Francisco: Benjamin Cummings, 2005.

Kerr, J., C. Winterford, and B. Harmon. "Cancer." *Cancer* 73 (1994): 2013–2026.

Kinoshita, J. "The Oncogene Connection." *Scientific American* 262 (1990): 24–25.

Kosta, L. "Multiplesensitivities." *Scientific American* 269 (1993): 10.

Leffell, D.J., and D.E. Brash. "Sunlight and Skin Cancer." *Scientific American* 275 (1996): 52–59.

Levy, M., R. Allsopp, A. Futcher, C. Greider, and C. Harley. "Telomere End-Replication Problem and Cell Aging." *Journal of Molecular Biology* 225 (1992): 951–960.

Lewin, B., L. Cassimeris, V. Lingappa, and G. Plopper. *Cells*. Sudbury, Mass.: Jones & Bartlett, 2006).

Lichenstein, L.M. "Allergy and the Immune System." *Scientific American* 269 (1993): 116–124.

Liotta, L.A. "Cancer Cell Invasion and Metastasis." *Scientific American* 266 (1992): 54–63.

Marguilis, L., and D. Sagan. *What Is Life?* Berkeley: University of California Press, 2000.

Marieb, E., and K.N. Hoehn. *Human Anatomy and Physiology.*7th ed. San Francisco: Benjamin Cummings, 2006.

Martindale, D. "Scar No More." *Scientific American* 283 (2000): 34–36.

Mazia, D. "The Cell Cycle." *Scientific American* 230 (1974): 53–64.

Molleman, A. *Patch Clamping: An Introductory Guide to Patch Clamp Electrophysiology.* West Sussex, England: Wiley, 2002.

Nakazawa, D., and D. Kerr. *The Autoimmune Epidemic.* New York: Touchstone, 2008.

Nicolaou, K.C., R.K. Guy, and P. Potier. "Toxoids: New Weapons Against Cancer." *Scientific American* 274 (1996): 94–98.

Noseworthy, J., C. Lucchinetti, M. Rodriguez, and B. Weinshenker. "Multiple Sclerosis." *New England Journal of Medicine* 343 (2000): 938–952.

Nucci, M.L., and A. Abuchowski. "The Search for Blood Substitutes." *Scientific American* 278 (1998): 72–77.

Oliff, A., J.B. Gibbs, and F. McCormick. "New Molecular Targets for Cancer Therapy." *Scientific American* 275 (1996): 144–149.

Parenteau, N. "Skin: The First Tissue-Engineered Products." *Scientific American* 280 (1999): 83–84.

Pedersen, R. "Embryonic Stem Cells for Medicine." *Scientific American* 280 (1999): 68–73.

Rennie, J. "The Body Against Itself." *Scientific American* 263 (1990): 106–115.

Ramaswamy, S., K. Ross, E. Lander, and T. Golub. "A Molecular Signature of Metastasis in Primary Solid Tumors." *Nature Genetics* 33 (2003): 49–54.

Ring, J., and T. Platts-Mills. *Allergy in Practice*. Berlin, N.Y.: Springer, 2005.

Rose, M.R. "Can Human Aging Be Postponed?" *Scientific American* 281 (1999): 106–111.

Rothman, J.E., and L. Orci. "Budding Vesicles in Living Cells." *Scientific American* 274 (1996): 70–75.

Rusting, R.L. "Hair: Why It Grows and Why It Stops." *Scientific American* 284 (2001): 70–79.

Sadava, D. *Cell Biology: Organelle Structure and Function*. Boston: Jones and Bartlett, 1993.

Saladin, K. *Anatomy and Physiology: The Unity of Form and Function*. 4th ed. New York: McGraw Hill, 2007.

Schmidt-Nielsen, K. *Scaling: Why Is Animal Size So Important?* New York: Cambridge University Press, 1984.

Sharon, N., and H. Lis. "Carbohydrates in Cell Recognition." *Scientific American* 268 (1993): 82–89.

Shier, D., J. Butler, and R. Lewis. *Hole's Essentials of Human Anatomy and Physiology*. 9th ed. Boston: McGraw Hill, 2005.

Skou, J.C. "The Na-K Pump." *News in Physiological Sciences* 7 (1992): 95–100.

Stein, W.D. *Channels, Carriers, and Pumps: An Introduction to Membrane Transport*. New York: Academic Press, 1990.

Stossel, T.P. "The Machinery of Cell Crawling." *Scientific American* (September 1994): 54–63.

Stryer, L., J.M. Berg, and J.L. Tymoczko. *Biochemistry*. 5th ed. San Francisco: Freeman, 2002.

Weinberg, R.A. "How Cancer Arises." *Scientific American* 275 (1996): 62–70.

Welsh, M.J., and A.E. Smith. "Cystic Fibrosis." *Scientific American* 273 (1995): 52–59.

Wu, C. "Unraveling the Mystery of Melanin: Does a Tan Protect Skin from Sun Damage or Contribute to It?" *Science News* 156 (1999): 190–191.

Further Resources

Web Sites

Acne.org:

http://www.acne.org

Acne, American Academy of Dermatology:

http://www.aad.org/pamphlets/acnepamp.html

American Cancer Society homepage:

http://www.cancer.org/docroot/home/index.asp

Antibiotics:

http://www.cs.stedwards.edu/chem/Chemistry/CHEM43/ CHEM43/Antibiotics/Antibiotics.HTML

Aquaporins:

http://fig.cox.miami.edu/~cmallery/150/memb/water. channels.htm

Aquaporin proteins—Water channels:

http://fig.cox.miami.edu/~cmallery/150/memb/water. channels.html

Bilirubin:

http://www.webmd.com/digestive-disorders/bilirubin-15434

Cell cycle and mitosis tutorial:

http://www.biology.arizona.edu/cell_bio/tutorials/cell_ cycle/main.html

Cell membranes, structure of:

http://telstar.ote.cmu.edu/biology/downloads/membranes/ index.html

Cell membranes, structure and function of:

http://cellbio.utmb.edu/cellbio/membrane.htm

http://users.rcn.com/jkimball.ma.ultranet/BiologyPages/C/ CellMembranes.html

Cell organelle, structure and function of:

http://www.tvdsb.on.ca/westmin/science/sbi3a1/Cells/cells. htm

Cell size:

http://staff.jccc.net/pdecell/cells/cellsize.html

Cell structures and functions:

http://library.thinkquest.org/12413/structures.html

Cell theory:

http://fig.cox.miami.edu/~cmallery150/unity/cell.text.htm

Cell—What is a cell?:

http://www.ncbi.nlm.nih.gov/About/primer/genetics_cell. html

Cells and organelles, cell cycle, mitosis—Images of:

http://www.cellsalive.com/

Cells—How cells function:

http://science.howstuffworks.com/cell.html

Cells—Transport into and out of cells:

http://www.emc.maricopa.edu/faculty/farabee/BIOBK/ BioBooktransp.html

Chemiosmosis:

http://www.life.uiuc.edu/crofts/bioph354/mitchell.html

Cold sores:

http://www.medicinenet.com/herpes_simplex_infections_ non-genital/article.htm

Diffusion and osmosis—Teaching unit:

http://biology.arizona.edu/sciconn/lessons/mccandless/ default.html

Endosymbiosis:

http://users.rcn.com/jkimball.ma.ultranet/BiologyPages/E/ Endosymbiosis.html

Epithelial tissues—Images:

http://www.uoguelph.ca/zoology/devobio/210labs/ epithelial1.html

Exocrine and endocrine glands:

http://www.mhhe.com/biosci/ap/histology_mh/glands.html

Free radicals and antioxidants:

http://www.healthchecksystems.com/antioxid.htm

Genes—What are genes?:

http://www.accessexcellence.org/AE/AEPC/NIH/gene03.php

Homeostasis:

http://www.bio-medicine.org/biology-definition/ Homeostasis/

Ion channels and membrane transport:

http://www.omedon.co.uk/ionchan/

Jaundice in newborns:

http://www.med.umich.edu/1libr/pa/pa_jaundnew_hhg. htm

Lysosomal storage disorders:

http://www.sas-centre.org/assays/genetic_enzymes/ lysstodisindex.html

Membrane structure and function:

http://www.cytochemistry.net/Cell-biology/membrane_ intro.htm

Membrane structure and transport:

http://www.emc.maricopa.edu/faculty/farabee/BIOBK/ BioBooktransp.html

Microscopes:

http://www.microbeworld.org/microbes/tools_microscopes. aspx

Microscopes, electron, source:

http://www.unl.edu/CMRAcfem/em.htm

Microscopes, kinds of:
http://nobelprize.org/educational_games/physics/microscopes/1.html

Microscopes, light:
http://www.ruf.rice.edu/~bioslabs/methods/microscopy/microscopy.html

Microscopes, light—How light microscopes work:
http://science.howstuffworks.com/light-microscope.htm

Microscopes, scanning electron—How scanning electron microscopes function:
http://www.mos.org/sln/SEM/

Nucleosome structure:
http://www.accessexcellence.org/RC/VL/GG/nucleosome.php

Nucleus:
http://cellbio.utmb.edu/cellbio/nucleus.html

Rosacea, cause of:
http://www.webmd.com/skin-problems-and-treatments/tc/rosacea-cause

Skin and connective tissue diseases:
http://www.mic.ki.se/Diseases/c17.html

Skin cancer, American Academy of Dermatology:
http://www.aad.org/SkinCancerNews/WhatIsSkinCancer/

Skin cancer, fact sheet about:
http://www.cdc.gov/cancer/nscpep/skin.htm

Skin cancer, introduction to:
http://www.maui.net/~southsky/introto.html#how

Stem cells—Source:
http://www.nih.gov/news/stemcell/primer.htm

Spontaneous generation:

http://www.accessexcellence.org/RC/AB/BC/Spontaneous_Generation.php

Taxol:

http://www.phcog.org/Taxus/Taxus_Web.html

Tay-Sachs disease:

http://ghr.nlm.nih.gov/condition=taysachsdisease

http://www.ninds.nih.gov/health_and_medical/disorders taysachs_doc.htm

Telomerase, aging, and cancer:

http://www.genethik.de/telomerase.htm

Warts:

http://dermatology.about.com/cs/warts/a/warts.htm

Picture Credits

Page

Index

About the Author

Douglas B. Light is an accomplished educator and holds degrees in biology (B.A.), zoology (M.S.), and physiology (Ph.D.). His academic career began at Winslow High School in Maine, where he taught biology. He joined the faculty at Ripon College in 1989 and taught general biology, anatomy and physiology, and immunology. He is currently a professor of biology at Lake Forest College, where he teaches courses in organismal biology and animal physiology. He also conducts research designed to elucidate the mechanisms regulating transport of substances across biological membranes and how cells maintain their proper size. He has received over a half dozen awards for his teaching and research excellence and has been the recipient of several major grants from the National Science Foundation. He has published over a dozen articles in scientific journals and has presented his research findings at numerous scientific conferences. Light is a member of several scientific and professional organizations, including the American Physiological Society, the Society for Integrative and Comparative Biology, and the Society of General Physiologists.

203321